IRISH SUPERSTITIONS AND LEGENDS
OF ANIMALS AND BIRDS

Irish Superstitions and Legends of Animals and Birds

PATRICK V. O'SULLIVAN

THE MERCIER PRESS

The Mercier Press Limited
4 Bridge Street, Cork
24 Lower Abbey Street, Dublin 1

© P. V. O'Sullivan, 1991

ISBN 0 85342 957 X

To animal lovers everywhere

Acknowledgements

The author and publisher wish to thank the Head of the Department of
Irish Folklore, University College Dublin for permission to publish
material from the archives of the Irish Folklore Commission.

Printed in Ireland by Litho Press Co., Midleton Co. Cork

Contents

Introduction

Why should you never ask a question of a dog? With what charms might you protect the cow house from influence of malevolent fairies and spirits? What would happen if you interfered with a swallow's nest? What were 'cuckoo oats'? Why are the first three days of April called 'the borrowed days'? Why should you never remove the shoes from a dead horse? Why were the hare and the hedgehog disliked in the pastures? What was significant when two hens began to fight? Why was the weasel described as 'the lady' or 'the noble lady'? What was the 'capall uisce'? Which animals did the fishermen not like to see when setting out for the strand? What happened when the mouse and the frog fell into the gallon of milk? How might you rid yourself of rats by writing them a letter? How might you effect a cure for baldness using the bladder of a goat? At what great Irish castle were foxes always seen before a death in the family? How might you cure an animal that had been overlooked by a neighbour with the evil eye? Why were the cows driven through a fire on Mid-Summer's Eve? Why was forge water held to have certain curative properties? How was the work of the churn protected? How did the cock outwit the fox? Why is the black hen smarter than the white hen? What did the eagle do when she found the soldier robbing her nest? Which bird was held to be sacred to St Brigid? Where did barnacle geese originate? How might you curse your neighbour's stock? From which bird did the wren learn its nest building techniques? What would happen if you saw a rook looking down the chimney? How did the wren betray the Irish? With which ear was it lucky to hear the cuckoo for the first time? What was the cure for red murrain in cattle? What are the three blessings of the cat? Why should you never bring the cat when moving to a new house? How would you make an aphrodisiac with the liver of a black cat? Why was the donkey a blessed animal? Why was it lucky to meet a white lamb first thing in the morning?

These questions and many, many more are about to be

answered in the following pages of superstitions concerning animals, riddles, folk cures, proverbs and tales.

Animals in Irish Mythology

Animals, both domestic and wild, have long co-existed side by side with mankind, and there are very few people who do not feel affection towards one kind of animal or another. The old saying that the dog is man's best friend has as much relevance today as in days gone by, but for generations animals were more than just friends and companions, as many of them played a central role in the rural economy of the country. Writing about 1930, H. V. Morton noted that the pig, the cow and the donkey were the props of the Irish countryside. Market days were frequent then, and there was much haggling over buying and selling, rows of donkey carts, many with saffron-coloured shafts, ranged along the narrow bustling street. These carts were generally laden with pigs, some fretful and squealing, some secure and slumbering. But this close association with animals extends even much further back than the day of the fair, for animals figured prominently in Irish mythology too – in the days of pre-history.

Cattle: The celebrated brown bull of Ulster lies at the heart of the tale of the Táin Bó Cuailgne. According to some versions of the story, King Aillil and Queen Medb of Connacht began to quarrel over the respective treasures that each one of them had brought to their marriage. 'It is well known,' said Medb to her husband, 'that my riches are more wonderful than yours.' 'This is a wonder to me,' retorted Aillil sharply,'for there is not a treasury of gold and jewels in Ireland that can compare with my own.' Their respective treasures were then brought forth and they were equal in all things save one – a beautiful white bull, the Fionnbheannach, the White-horned. This bull had been born in Medb's herd but it had defected to that of Aillil, as it did not wish to be subject to a woman. Medb had no match for this handsome animal and she became so frustrated that all her riches seemed as nothing to her. Yet she determined she would find a bull to rival the Fionnbheannach, and soon she heard news of the existence of the magnificent Donn or brown bull of Cuailgne, which belonged to one called Daire.

The queen of Connacht sent messengers to Daire offering him the most fabulous riches in return for the bull. At first, Daire was quite willing to part with his much prized animal. Later, however, the emissaries from Connacht indulged too liberally in the ales provided by Daire and his household, and they foolishly boasted that if Daire had not agreed to part with the bull voluntarily they would have wrested it from him by main force. Daire was suitably offended and vowed by the gods that if Medb and her cohorts wished to have the Donn of Cuailgne, they would indeed have to take the beast from him by force. Thus began the war for the celebrated bull. At the end of this long and colourful saga, the two bulls, the Fionnbheannach and the Donn, engaged in deadly conflict, after which the brown bull came over the hill of Crúachain with the remnants of his noble adversary transfixed through his horns.

Soon afterwards the brown bull returned to Cuailgne but, when he reached his native place, he collapsed on the hillside, giving three resonant mournful bellows that echoed all around. Blood came gushing from his mouth, and he died.

There are, in fact, several Táin-type tales, or tales of cattle raids, in Irish mythology, amongst them the Táin Bó Dartada, the Táin Bó Flidias and, perhaps the best known apart from the Táin Bó Cuailgne, the Táin Bó Fraoch.

According to some mythological traditions, the first cows were brought to Ireland by a beautiful maiden from the sea. She brought with her three sacred cows – Bó Finn, the white cow, Bó Ruadh, the red cow, and Bó Dubh, the black cow – and it is from these three cows that all the cows in Ireland are ultimately descended. When the cows emerged from the sea they each took a different course; the black cow headed south, the red went northwards, while the magnificent Bó Finn traced her steps towards the royal residence at Tara. Every place the Bó Finn lingered was named after her – hence such evocative place names as Lough na Bó Finn (the lake of the white cow) and Tobar Bó Finn (the well of the white cow). The white cow gave birth to two beautiful calves, and when she had done this she vanished into a cave beside the sea, a cave which is unknown to mankind. There the fabulous cow remains to this day; there she sleeps her enchanted sleep, nor shall be roused from that fairy slumber until the rightful king of Ireland comes to waken her. Later versions stated that the white cow was struck down by a red-haired woman. This was the age of the allegory, and so the white cow represented Ireland while the red-haired woman was Queen Elizabeth I.

The great mythological battle, the Second Battle of Mag Tuiread, was fought between the Tuatha Dé Danann and their arch enemies the Fomóir. Bres, the beautiful, one of the Fomóir, had been chosen as King of the Tuatha Dé in the hope that this would help to cement an alliance which had existed between the two sides. Bres' rule, however, was oppressive and unjust and he obliged the Dagda, the god of Druidism and the father of all the gods, to build a fort for him. Part of the original text reads:

> Then the Dagda brought his work to an end and Bres asked what he would take as wages for his labour. The Dagda answered. 'I require that you gather the cattle of Ireland in one place'. The King did as he asked and he chose a heifer from amongst them. This seemed foolish to Bres for he thought that the Dagda might have chosen something more.

The Fomóir were defeated by the Tuatha Dé and, after the battle, the Dagda brought forth his heifer. The heifer began to low to her calf and that lowing summoned back all the cattle of Ireland which the Fomóir had demanded as tribute during the kingship of the malevolent Bres.

In Irish mythology the goddess Bóann was the goddess of the white cow, and the colours of her cattle were said to symbolise the different phases of the moon. The river Boyne is named after her. She was sometimes listed as the wife of the water god Neictean and sometimes as the wife of Elcmar the Divine. She had a secret tryst with the Dagda and later gave birth to Aengus, the god of love.

White cows with red ears were not real animals, rather were they enchanted creatures. Fraoch, the central character in the Táin Bó Fraoch, and reputedly the most handsome warrior in Ireland, was the son of Bé Find, sister of the goddess Bóann. In the Táin Bó Fraoch we read: 'And twelve fine cows his mother gave to him and white they were with red ears.' When the raven goddess, the Mórrigan was rejected by Cúchulainn she attacked him in the guise of a white heifer with red ears, when the hero was engaged in single combat with Loch.

* * *

Horses: If there were enchanted cattle there were also enchanted horses as illustrated by this description of the raven goddess and her chariot:

> There came a chariot harnessed with a chestnut horse. The horse had but one leg and the pole of the chariot passed through its body, so that the peg in front met the halter passing across its forehead. Within the chariot was a woman, her eyebrows red and a crimson mantle round her. Her mantle fell behind her between the wheels of the chariot so that it swept along the ground.

Two of the most celebrated horses in Irish mythology were the Grey of Macha and the Black of Sanglu, both born at the time of the birth of Cúchulainn. These newly born foals were presented as gifts to the baby boy. The grey of Macha also figured prominently in the tale of Cúchulainn's death. The goddess Mórrigan came and broke a wheel on the hero's chariot during the night, in an effort to prevent him from travelling to his last battle. Cúchulainn ordered Laeg, the charioteer, to yoke the chariot but the majestic horse resisted all attempts at being harnessed. Laeg interpreted this uncharacteristic wilfulness on the part of the horse as an omen. When Cúchulainn drew near, the Grey of Macha turned his left side three times towards his master. 'You have never behaved like this before,' Cúchulainn said reproachfully, and then the noble horse came by him and began to shed mournful tears of deep dark blood. In that last battle, Erc, the King of Leinster, cast his spear at Cúchulainn but it pierced the noble body of the Grey. Cúchulainn withdrew the spear and then the wounded steed galloped away with part of the shattered harness dangling about him. When Cúchulainn himself was mortally wounded, the faithful horse returned to defend him, making an onslaught against his master's enemies, killing fifty of them with his teeth and thirty of them with his hoofs.

One of the most amusing tales in the Ossianic cycle is the story of the Giolla Deacair and his horse. Abarta, also known as the Giolla Deacair, came amongst the Fianna with a great, grey, scrawny, ill-tempered nag. When the Giolla's horse was released amongst the horses of the Fianna he began to attack them savagely, kicking them and biting them so that they streamed with blood. Conán Maol clambered onto the horse's back but the animal refused to budge. The gallant Conán was suitably mortified at his lack of success, the men of the Fianna falling about with fits of laughter, some of them wondering if

Conán had become horse boy to the giant.

Then it was suggested that the horse did not move simply because it was accustomed to carry much greater weight. One by one the men of the Fianna clambered onto the horse's back until, at last, fourteen of them were astride the scrawny steed. The Giolla indignantly expressed himself outraged at the unseemly manner in which his noble steed had been treated, and so he turned and strode away. Soon he was racing across hill and plain with his horse galloping close behind, the fourteen men of the Fianna still on the horse's back, and a fifteenth grasping unceremoniously at the animal's tail. Later Fionn was furnished with a ship, and he followed the trail of the Giolla Deacair's horse across the sea until, at last, he and his fellows came to the Otherworld. Messengers were sent to Abarta advising him that if he did not promptly release the prisoners, the Fianna would wage war upon himself and his subjects. The Giolla repented, inviting Fionn and his warriors to a great feast where they were reunited with their long absent comrades who had been carried away from them. Fionn was willing to accept the Giolla's expressions of regret, but Conán Maol demanded some reparation. At length it was decided that fourteen of the Giolla's men should clamber onto the horse's back and that the Giolla himself should grasp the horse's tail. In this manner should they make their way to Ireland so that they might endure some of the ignominy which had been perpetrated on Conán and his companions. When they returned to Ireland the Giolla by some enchantment contrived to make the horses of the Fianna well again. Then he and his fellows disappeared without trace and were never seen again. Gone too was the ill-tempered horse that had been the cause of all the trouble.

Tales of voyages were very popular. One of the best-loved tales of this genre was 'The Voyage of Maeldun'. Amongst the many strange and exotic islands visited by Maeldun and his companions was the island of the giant horses. Those sent ashore to explore the sinister island came upon an enormous racecourse bearing the prints of horse hoofs of monstrous size. The scouts returned to the boat and the voyagers sailed swiftly away. They had gone but a little distance when they saw a race of giant horses in progress, great multitudes of shadowy forms cheering on their own favourites and it seemed to Maeldun that these were not earthly creatures, but demons.

* * *

Dogs: Many of the tales in Irish mythology focus on the activities of noblemen and warriors who were constantly engaged in what was seen as one of the most noble pursuits of the countryside – that of hunting. Both hounds and deer are frequently mentioned in these tales and perhaps the most celebrated hounds of all were Bran and Sceolan, the enchanted hounds of Fionn Mac Cumhaill. One text records that these hounds were of strange breed. Fionn's aunt Tuireann was married to Ullan and she discovered that he was having an affair with a druidess. Ullan's jealous lover turned Turieann into a she-dog and thus she bore the hounds Bran and Sceolan. One day when Fionn and his hounds were out hunting on the Hill of Allen, the hounds startled a fawn. The hounds gave chase but when they at length overtook their quarry they began to frolic about her and lick her face. Observing this curious behaviour, Fionn ordered that the fawn should not be killed and they brought her back with them to their dún. That night the fawn changed into a beautiful woman, Sadb, telling Fionn that she had been turned into a fawn by the Dark Druid when she had refused to give her love to him. Sadb remained with Fionn and they were lovers. One day Fionn was called away and in his absence the Dark Druid came upon Sadb, and smote her with his wand, whereupon she reverted into the shape of a fawn once more. When he returned, Fionn searched far and wide but could find no trace of his beloved Sadb, until one day on Ben Bulben he chanced upon a naked boy. He took the boy home with him and discovered that he had been reared by a fawn. Fionn knew then that this was his own son, born of Sadb, and the name he gave to the child was Oisín which means 'Little Fawn'.

There are, in fact, several tales of huntings and enchantments in the Ossianic cycle, but there are also vivid hunting passages in the tales of the Ulster Cycle, such as this one from the Táin Bó Fraoch:

> Then it was that the hosts came out from the royal fort of Crúachain to meet their guests and there was such a great multitude that not a few amongst them suffocated and died. The newcomers dismounted close to the door of Medb's dún whereupon they unbridled their horses and let loose the hounds; the hounds hunted seven deer to the Rath of Crúachain, seven foxes and seven hares and seven wild boars too, and the warriors struck them down on the lawns before the fort. After this the hounds jumped into the river, bringing forth

seven otters and taking them too to the doorway of Medb's dún.

The *geis* was an important feature of many tales in Irish mythology. It was essentially a prohibition which precluded the subject from engaging in certain specified activities. One of the *geasa* on Cúchulainn was that he should not eat the flesh of the dog, from whom he derived his name (the hound of Culainn), while another insisted that he should not pass a cooking hearth without partaking of some of the fare. On his way to his last battle, he encountered three hags, all blind in the left eye, and they were cooking a venomous dog on spits made of rowan. 'Stay awhile,' one of the hags called to him but the hero declined her invitation. 'If we had finer fare than a humble hound, then would you stop to eat with us,' the hag retorted vindictively. Cúchulainn yielded at length. The hag handed him a shoulder blade of the hound. He took it with his left hand and ate of it before placing it beside his left thigh. In an instant both hand and thigh had withered and had lost their strengths.

* * *

Pigs: The wild boar plays a significant role in the colourful world of Irish mythology. Fled Ghoibhnenn was the Otherworld Feast and was presided over by the god Goibhniú. Here was served a magical ale, and all who drank of it were rendered immune from death and disease. The meat of enchanted pigs was served at the meal for, though the pigs might be slaughtered and eaten one day, they were alive and well the next day ready to face the same unpleasant fate again and again. The honour of carving the boar was the major bone of contention in Bricriú's feast or Fled Bricrend. Bricriú was one of the nobles of Ulster and his epithet was *Neamhtheanga*, which means bitter tongue, for he was ever intent on creating strife and dissension amongst his companions. Bricriú invited to his feast the three great heroes of Ulster – Cúchulainn, Conall Cearnach and Laegaire Buadach. He incited each of them to claim the champion's portion at the feast for they might then rightly claim to be the champion of champions of all the Ulster men. Inevitably the heroes came to blows at the feast, and when this uproar was quelled by King Conchobar and Sencha, the peacemaker, Bricriú then contrived to set the wives of the heroes against one another. The ladies and their attendants went outside for a little while after the discord amongst their husbands, Bricriú telling them in turn that the first of them to return to the.dún would be queen of the entire province of Ulster. It was eventually decided that the heroes should set forth for Rath Crúachain, the royal dún of King Aillil and Queen Medb of Connacht and that the issue should be decided by Aillil.

Medb dominated her ineffectual husband in most of the tales from the Ulster Cycle, and so, when Aillil procrastinated and could not come to a decision, his wife chided him:

'It is a weakling you are. You have been chosen as a judge so give judgment.'

Aillil retorted feebly that the heroes were so evenly matched it was impossible to decide amongst them and besides, he would get no thanks whichever judgment he gave.

'It is not a difficult matter to me to judge them,' said Medb, 'Laegaire and Conall Cearnach are as different as bronze and white gold, while Conall and Cúchulainn are as different as white gold and red gold.'

Thus the judgment at Crúachain was given to Cúchulainn, but again Laegaire and Conall would not accept the decision. At length Cúchulainn was obliged to do battle with a giant to prove his superiority.

Bricriú was also cast in the familiar role of troublemaker in the tale of Mac Datho's pig. The tale reveals one obvious similarity to the tale of the Táin Bó Cuailgne. In the Táin the provinces of Ulster and Connacht go to war over the fabulous bull, the Donn of Cuailgne, while in Mac Datho's Pig they come to blows over the magnificent hound, Ailbe, owned by Mesrioda Mac Datho. Messengers came to Mac Datho from Connacht and from Ulster, each party earnestly requesting that the hound should be given to them in return for which the Leinster king would receive many precious gifts. Mac Datho was in something of a quandary. He did not want to offend either of the neighbouring provinces. Then, on the prompting of his astute wife, he took the messengers from Connacht and the messengers from Ulster aside in turn, telling them that after much serious reflection he had decided to give the dog to them. Furthermore, he invited Aillil and Medb of Connacht and King Conchobar of Ulster to come and collect the hound on the same day.

Mac Datho, it appears, was a consummate actor for he blithely expressed great surprise when the men of Connacht and the men of Ulster appeared together on his doorstep on the day appointed, but recovering himself from the shock he invited them all inside and welcomed them warmly. MacDatho had slaughtered a stupendous pig which had been nurtured for seven years on the milk of seven milch cows, and when it was served forty oxen were laid across it. There arose a dispute as to how the magnificent specimen should be served, and Bricriú promptly suggested that it should be divided in proportion to the battle honour of both provinces. Cet of Connacht insisted that he himself was the bravest of all those present and that he would carve the pig. When one by one the men of Ulster sought to challenge him, Cet silenced each of them with a tale of some humiliation he had personally inflicted upon them. Finally Conall Cearnach arrived, demanding that Cet should abandon his place by the pig, for not a single day had passed that Conall had not killed a warrior of Connacht; not a single night he had not slept with the head of a Connacht man under his knee. 'You are better than I, that is true,' admitted Cet, 'but if our champion, Anluan, were here, he would do battle with you.' Thereupon Conall took the bloodied head of Anluan from his belt and flung it at his adversary, blood bursting from the lips of the severed head.

Conall began to carve the pig, reserving the leanest and most tender portions for his Ulster comrades while at the same time offering only the foretrotters to the men of Connacht. The warriors of Connacht were suitably offended and a fracas erupted. This soon spilled onto the courtyard. Mac Datho loosed his hound, and Ailbe chose to side with the men of Ulster who had soon routed their adversaries, but Fer Loga, the royal charioteer of Aillil and Medb, swept after the dog in his chariot, smashing its head with the chariot pole. The place where this incident occurred was called Mag nAilbi, sometimes called the plain of Ailbe.

It was a wild boar which caused the death of the handsome Diarmuid in one of the most celebrated tales of the Ossianic cycle, 'Tóraíocht Diarmuid agus Grania', but hounds also play their part. Diarmuid, son of Donn, was fostered by Aengus Óg, the God of Love, at his residence at Brugh na Boinne. Donn discovered that his wife was unfaithful to him and soon she bore another child by Roc, the steward of Aengus. When this child was quite young, he fled from some fighting hounds and sought refuge between the knees of Donn, but the embittered Donn crushed him to death and then cast the body amongst the hounds on the floor. Later, Roc took an enchanted rod and smote the body of the dead child with it, transforming it into a fierce boar of immense size. Roc prophesied that the boar would bring about the death of Diarmuid.

Diarmuid was known as Diarmuid of the Love Spot, and both a sheep and a cat figure in the tale that explains how he acquired that celebrated mark. He was out hunting with his three companions, Goll, Conán and Oscar. Late at night they came to a modest hut in the wood where they found an old man, a young girl, a wether sheep and a cat. They were made welcome but, when they sat down to eat, the wether leapt onto the table and the huntsmen could not move it. The old man bade the cat lead the wether away and tie it up, explaining to his guests that the wether was the world and the cat was the cat of death which had the power to destroy the world. The four companions went to bed in a spacious room, the young girl coming to sleep in the same room with them, her beauty as radiant as the light of a candle. Each of the men came to her and wished to make love to her, but she rejected the advances of the first three. She did not refuse Diarmuid and she said to him: 'I am youth and I shall put a mark on you so that no woman can ever see you without loving you'. She reached out and touched his forehead and bestowed on Diarmuid his celebrated love spot.

Much later Diarmuid went hunting with Fionn and the Fianna on the slopes of Ben Bulben where they encountered the enchanted boar that was Diarmuid's stepbrother. Diarmuid loosed his hound, but the hound fled in terror. He then slung a stone which struck the boar directly in the middle of the forehead, but it did not impede the progress of the enchanted beast. The boar drew nearer and Diarmuid lashed at him with his sword, but the sword splintered in two. Then the boar rushed at the hero, goring him and ripping out his bowels, but Diarmuid retaliated by implanting the shaft of his sword in the brain of his adversary. The exultant Fionn, who had hated Diarmuid ever since the fateful day of his elopement with the beautiful Grania, came and stood over the dying Diarmuid. 'It likes me well to see thee in that plight, O Diarmuid,' he said. 'And I would that all the women in Ireland could see thee now, for thy excellent beauty is turned to ugliness and thy manly form to deformity.' Diarmuid begged Fionn to heal his wounds with a draught of water from his hands. Fionn went to a well nearby, but before he came to Diarmuid he let the water trickle through his fingers. He went to the well a second time, and a second time the water trickled through his fingers. Fionn went a third time, but, before he had brought the water close to the lips of the dying hero, the life had departed from the breast of the handsome Diarmuid.

* * *

Cats: If Labhraid Loinseach, King of Leinster, had the ears of a horse then the usurper Cairbre Cathcheann had the ears of a cat. He was a leader of the Aitheath Tuatha, a people who predated the Milesians. They rebelled against their Milesian overlords, and Cairbre unlawfully seized the kingship. This violated the sacred character of the office, and so during Cairbre's reign there was only one grain on each stalk of corn and one acorn on each oak. The rivers were without fish and the cattle without milk.

Guaire Aidne, King of Connacht, was known as Guaire the generous, and on one occasion the chief bard, Sencha Mac Aillil, and a large band of his companions imposed themselves on Guaire's household. They were treated with every kindness but still they carped and moaned interminably. Sencha declared petulantly that he had never stomached such unpalatable food in his entire life and he could not be tempted to partake of the fine fare offered to him. The king dreaded the power of the bards for they could satirise himself and his household with their words. Then one day a pretty young serving girl offered to bring the sulking bard a hen egg and, being half famished, he bade her set it before him. She returned with the sad news that the egg was nowhere to be found, that it had been carried off by the mice, the nimble race. Sencha felt suitably aggrieved and immediately chanted a satire so venomous against all mice that ten of the hapless creatures fell dead at his feet during the course of his invective

Then he pondered further on the matter and came to the conclusion that the cat was indeed more culpable than the mice for it was the duty of the cat to keep the mice at bay, and he had lamentably failed in that task. Thereupon, Sencha launched forth with another satire against the race of cats and most particularly against their overlord, Irusan, a cat of monstrous size who dwelt in a cave near Knowth on the river Boyne. The bard described how the otter had bitten off the ears of the progenitor of cats so that ever since that time every cat had jagged ears, and he added: 'Irusan, let your tail hang down for the mouse leers and jeers at your kind.' The great cat in his cave heard these unkindly words, and promptly set out for the court of Guaire where he soon inspired terror in the hearts of all those who chanced to gaze upon him, for he was the size of a bull, his eyes shining with rage, his sharpened claws protruding ominously from his feet. Irusan grabbed Sencha and carried him off on his back, the repentant bard attempting to make amends by flattering the gigantic cat as it swept through the countryside. St Ciarán of Clonmacnoise happened to observe Sencha's predicament and the saint, thinking that the bard had been wretchedly treated by Guaire and had been expelled by him, rushed at the great cat and struck it with an iron bar which he had taken from a forge. The cat fell dead but Sencha was less than grateful to the saint for his intervention. He would have preferred if Irusan had eaten him so that the entire episode might bring much discredit on Guaire, for Sencha would not have found himself in such a wretched plight if it had not been for Guaire's unsavoury meals.

The chief bard and the king were reconciled in time and in another tale, Sencha comes face to face with the ghost of Fergus Mac Roich, one of the noble warriors of Ulster, and Fergus narrates the celebrated tale of the Táin Bó Cuailgne.

One of the islands visited by Maeldun and his companions in the voyage of Maeldun was the island of the little cat. Here was a great white palace with four stone columns in one of the spacious apartments. A cat leapt from the top of one column to the next. The chamber was filled with treasures of every kind – brooches and torques and swords displayed upon the walls – and here too was an abundance of fine food and drink. The newcomers ate and drank and slept awhile. Next day as they prepared to leave, one of Maeldun's foster brothers took a necklace from the wall. The cat leapt at him like a fiery dart and he fell in a pile of ashes on the floor. Maeldun, who had forbidden the theft, calmed the cat, restored the necklace and scattered the ashes of his dead foster brother on the shore of the island of the little cat.

Birds in Irish Mythology

The most celebrated bird in Irish mythology must surely be the swan. The children of Lir, Fionnuala and Aedh, Fiachra and Conn, were transformed into swans by their jealous stepmother, Aoife. Under this terrible enchantment they were obliged to spend three hundred years on Loch Dairbhreach, three hundred years on Sruth na Maoile and three hundred years at Irrus Domnann and Inis Gluaire. When the treacherous Aoife cast her spell upon her stepchildren she said:

> Out out, upon the waters child swans of Lir
> Fortune smiles not on your days of glory
> Well may your friends bewail your fate
> With clamorous birds shall be your doom.

The children of Lir still retained their capacity to speak, and while they remained on the sheltered waters of Loch Dairbhreach, they could take some little comfort from the society of their friends, but at length they were obliged to take their leave of these friends and make their abode on the dark and raging waters of Sruth na Maoile. Fionnuala sang:

> Away my brothers from Dairbhreach's wave
> On the wings of the southern wind.
> We leave our father and our friends today
> In measureless grief behind.
> Ah, sad the parting and sad our flight
> To Moyle's tempestuous main
> For the day of woe shall come and go
> before we meet again.

At the end of nine hundred years the swans heard the Christian bell for the first time on Inis Gluaire. The saint who had made his abode on the island took care of them and instructed them in the ways of the new faith. Lairgnen was king of Connacht at that time and he was married to Decca of Munster. Decca wished to have the singing swans for herself, for wonderful tales of the fabulous birds had reached her ears. The holy man, however, would not part with the swans and, when the indignant Lairgnen tried to drag the birds from the altar of the little church on the island of Inis Gluaire, they reverted to human form once more; three decrepit old men and a haggard old woman. The children of Lir died soon afterwards, having been baptised in the Christian faith.

Another very beautiful tale is Aisling Aengusa, the dream of Aengus. Aengus was the god of Love, the son of the Dagda and the goddess, Bóann. His foster father was Midir of Brí Leith. Aengus had a dream in which he saw a stunningly beautiful young woman, and he fell passionately in love with that vision of loveliness. Fergne, the physician, advised the lovesick Aengus to seek the aid of his mother, Bóann. A search was made throughout Ireland for a year, but to no avail – the bewitching creature that had so tantalisingly stalked the love god's dreams could not be traced. Next, the Dagda was consulted, then the god Bodb Dearg, 'For his knowledge spreads through Ireland.' Some of Bodb Dearg's men eventually came upon the fair one at Loch Bel Dracon in Cruit Cliath. Aengus was summoned to Loch Bel Dracon and he instantly recognised the woman of his dreams amidst a host of thrice fifty girls, each pair of them linked by a silver chain.

Then Bodb Dearg identified the maiden as Caer Ibormeith, daughter of Ethel Anbuail from Sid Uamuin in the province of Connacht. Messengers were sent to Connacht, but King Aillil and Queen Medb had no power over Caer and neither had her father, Ethel Anbuail. Ethel disclosed however that his daughter spent one year in the shape of a bird and the subsequent year in human form once more. The following Samhain (ancient festival of first of November) she would take the shape of a swan on Loch Bel Dracon with thrice fifty swans round about her. Aengus went to the lake at Samhain and there he saw the beautiful snow white birds with their silver chains and golden crowns. 'Come to me. Come to me, Caer,' Aengus called out from the lake shore. She retorted that she would come to him if he promised that she might return to the lake. He gave his word, then he placed his arms about her and slept with her in the form of a swan. Then they circled the lake three times, which the cunning Aengus regarded as the fulfilment of his promise. Thereafter they flew to the royal residence at Brúgh na Boinne where they sang in such mellifluous tones that the people there fell asleep for three days and three nights. Thus the tale of Aengus and Caer had a happy ending.

In the tale of the wooing of Etain, the god Midir, foster father of

Aengus, fell in love with Etain Echraidhe, daughter of Aillil Echraidhe. Aengus helped his foster father to win the hand of the winsome Etain, and soon Midir returned with her to Brí Leith. Here his first wife, Fuamnach, became insanely jealous of the newcomer, striking her with an enchanted rod and turning her into a pool of water, which soon developed into a worm, and then into a majestic purple fly, and the music of the fly was the sweetest music in the world. Midir knew that this was Etain so the fly was always in his company. Fuamnach conjured up an enchanted wind which swept the hapless fly out to sea where it remained for seven years before alighting on the breast of Aengus at Brúgh na Boinne.

Aengus carried the beautiful fly about in a sunny bower made of shimmering crystal, but it was not long before the jealous Fuamnach heard of the return of the fly and saw to it that Etain was swept away by another violent blast of fairy wind. Over a thousand years later, the fly fell into a golden cup and was swallowed by the wife of Etar who soon became pregnant and gave birth to Etain, daughter of Etar. Later Eochaidh Airemh, the High King of Ireland, married the bewitching Etain, but one day Midir came to the King on the ramparts at Tara. They played Ficheall, a game like chess, and at first Eochaidh was the winner of game after game, Midir rewarding his successes with the valuable stakes they had agreed upon. At length, Midir suggested they should play another game, the winner choosing his own stake. Midir duly won and told of his wish: 'My arms around Etain and a kiss from her lips.' The High King resented this brazen request but bade Midir return in one month's time. On the appointed day, Eochaidh had all the doors of his court securely locked while his warriors encircled the royal dún of Tara. Yet, much to the astonishment of the company, Midir appeared before them in the midst of the banqueting hall. Then he placed his arms around Etain in the centre of the room, and together they rose up through the roof, whereupon they took the form of two swans and flew off into the distance.

Having wasted a year digging up almost every fairy mound in Ireland, Eochaidh and his men rode to Brí Leith, Midir's home, and laid siege to it, but Midir appeared to them, telling the High King that his wife would be restored to him at the third hour of the next day. The following morning, however, fifty young maidens, each in the form and dress of Etain, came before Eochaidh who found himself in something of a quandary. Eventually he chose one of them. This was not Etain, but

Etain Óg – daugher of Etain and his daughter too, but Eochaidh slept with his daughter and she bore him a child before he heard of his terrible mistake.

This child, a daughter called Mess Buachalla, went on to marry the High King, Eterscel and she bore him a son Conaire Mór. According to some versions of the tale, the mysterious bird-god, Nemglan, came to Mess Buachalla and made love to her on the eve of her marriage to Eterscel. On the death of the High King, Nuadua Necht, a great flock of birds flew low over Conaire's chariot. The birds were marvellously coloured and Conaire took his sling to make a cast at one of them, but suddenly they were transformed into handsome warriors. One of them introduced himself as his father, telling Conaire that he must never make a cast at birds for they were his own kind. It had been prophesied that the next high king would come naked along the road to Tara, and so Nemglan, privy to this secret knowledge, told his son to walk naked into Tara, where he was received with great joy and was duly installed as king.

A flock of beautiful birds devastated the lands around Emhain Macha, the royal residence of King Conchobar, before the birth of Cúchulainn. The men of Ulster were fascinated not only by the beauty of the birds, but also by the sweetness of their singing. One day they yoked their chariots and pursued the great flock, Conchobar's daughter, Dechtire, serving as charioteer for her father. There were nine flights of birds in all, a score in each flight, and each pair of birds was linked by a silver chain. After dusk three birds broke away from the others and directed their course towards Brúgh na Boinne. The shades of night came down upon the Ulster men, and snow began to swirl in dense clouds about them. Conchobar sent messengers to seek shelter. They came to a house inhabited by a couple, and the entire party was made welcome, the man of the house explaining that his wife was in labour. Dechtire went to lend what assistance she could, and soon the woman had given birth to a baby boy. At the same time a mare outside the house gave birth to twin foals, and the man gave the foals as a gift to the newborn child.

When morning came, however, the birds and the house had vanished; there was nothing to be seen by the men of Ulster except their own horses, the baby boy and the foals. They took the child back to Emhain Macha, where Dechtire nursed and reared him, until one day, to her great sadness, the boy fell ill and died. When she had shed her bitter tears of grief she felt thirsty and was given a copper vessel, but each time she drew the vessel close to her mouth a tiny creature leapt into her mouth with the liquid. That night she had a dream in which she saw the god, Lug, who told her that it was he who had lured her to Brúgh na Boinne and it was his house she had entered there. The child who had died had been his son, but now Lug would enter her womb and would cause her to become pregnant. The men of Ulster were greatly perplexed when they saw Dechtire with child. How was this possible they muttered? Had her father made incestuous love to her while in some drunken stupor? For it was known that Dechtire slept next to him.

Conchobar betrothed his daughter to Suldaim Mac Rioch, but she felt greatly ashamed that she should have to go to her husband's bed as a pregnant woman; so when the time of birth was close at hand she lay upon her swollen stomach and pressed hard, crushing the child within her womb. Then she went to Suldaim's bed and soon she was with child by him. Thereafter, she bore him a son who was at first named Setanta, and later Cúchulainn.

The Boyhood Deeds of Cúchulainn feature an episode describing the hero's encounter with the fierce sons of Nechta Scéine. When he had slaughtered all three of them he severed their heads and brought them back to the chariot which was driven by Ibor, King Conchobar's charioteer. On the way back to Emhain, Cúchulainn captured a deer which he fastened to the back of the chariot. Then they chanced upon a flock of beautiful swans, and Cúchulainn wondered if it would win him more glory to take some of the swans back with him alive or dead. Alive, the charioteer Ibor assured him without hesitation. Cúchulainn made a cast at the birds with a stone, bringing down large numbers of them without killing them. When the charioteer had collected the swans, Cúchulainn loosely secured them to the chariot with cords so that they might fly low overhead. It was in this manner that the young hero returned to Emhain – the graceful swans on the wing above the chariot, the severed heads proudly displayed as battle trophies, and the fleet-footed deer racing along behind the chariot. Now Cúchulainn was overwhelmed with the ardour of battle, and in that state he could not distinguish between friend and foe. King Conchobar decided on a novel response to the approaching danger. 'Send naked women to greet him,' he insisted. This was done and amongst those who bared their breast was Conchobar's own wife, the queen Mugan.

Cúchulainn was suitably embarrassed and, when he turned his face away, the men of Ulster grabbed him and plunged him into a vat of cold water. The first vat fell asunder with the intensity of the heat; the water in the second vat bubbled and seethed; and, though the water in the third vat was heated too, the heat was not immoderate. Soon the hero was calm again and, when he emerged from the third vat, he was dressed in rich robes and brought before the King.

Birds are also very much part of the tale of the Wasting Sickness of Cúchulainn. One time at Samhain when there was an assembly at Emhain Macha, a flock of beautiful birds descended upon a nearby lake. The women of Ulster greatly desired them, wishing they might have a pair of the fabulous birds, one for each shoulder. Cúchulainn captured the birds and distributed them amongst the women but then found that there was none left for his own wife. She was not angry, however, and the hero promised that if more birds came upon the lake, he would capture two of the most beautiful for her. Soon two beautiful birds linked with a golden chain were seen about the lake and the song they sang brought sleep upon the hosts.

His wife urged Cúchulainn not to pursue the birds, fearing that they possessed some strange powers. Cúchulainn set out after the birds, but though his spear pierced the wing of one of them he was unable to catch them, and they disappeared under the shimmering silver waters of the lake. The hero walked on for some time, then rested with his back to a pillar stone. He fell asleep and in his dreams two women, one dressed in crimson, the other in green, came and lashed him with a horsewhip and left him almost lifeless. Cúchulainn was taken to An Teach Breac, the speckled house, and remained there in his sickness for a year.

When Samhain came around again, a stranger who identified himself as Aengus, son of Aed Abrat, came to An Teach Breac and invited Cúchulainn to Mag Cruach, which was in the Otherworld, where the stranger's sister, Fand, pined with love and longing to have the hero by her side. Cúchulainn then made his way to the pillar stone where he encountered again one of the women he had seen in the vision the year before. She was Lí Ban, wife of Labhraid Luath Lámh, who reigned in Mag Mell, the plain of delights. She explained that if Cúchulainn consented to fight for a single day with Labhraid against his enemies, his health would be restored and he would win the love of the bewitching Fand. Cúchulainn then sent his charioteer, Laeg, with Lí Ban so that he might bring back news of her homeland. Laeg returned with marvellous tales of his adventure in the Otherworld, but Cúchulainn's wife, Emer, scolded her husband saying that he had been brought low by his infatuation for a woman he had seen in a vision; that was the reason for his lethargy and he would never recover until he roused himself from that lethargy.

Laeg travelled a second time with Lí Ban, and when he returned he was again filled with admiration for the marvels and splendours of Mag Mell, the plain of delights. It was after this that Cuchulainn went to that wondrous place and, having defeated Labhraid's enemies, he became the lover of Fand with whom he remained a month. They arranged to meet again at Ibor Ci Trátha, but Emer learned of this rendezvous and confronted Cúchulainn with his infidelity. Mannanan Mac Lir, God of the Sea and the consort of Fand, came to the same place and, when Fand agreed to return with him, he shook his cloak between the hero and his lover so that they might never again meet in time. Thereafter, the druids gave a draught of forgetfulness to Cuchulainn and to Emer so that Cúchulainn might forget his great love for Fand and so that Emer might forget her jealousy.

Weather Lore

In the days before satellite stations and weather charts, the people of the countryside looked for signs in nature to help them determine the kind of weather that was near at hand. Old people often recited parts of this poem which gauged the behaviour of animals and birds as signals of approaching rain.

> The hollow winds begin to blow
> The clouds look black, the glass is low.
> The soot falls down and spaniels sleep
> And spiders from their cobweb creep.
> Last night the moon went pale to bed
> The moon in hollows hid her head;
> The brooding shepherd heaves a sigh
> For see a rainbow spans the sky.
> The walls are damp, the ditches smell
> Closed is the pink-eyed pimpernel;
> Hark, how the chairs and tables crack
> Old Betty's joints are on the rack.
> Loud quack the ducks and peacocks cry
> The distant hills are looking nigh.
> How restless are the snorting swine
> The busy flies disturb the kine.
> Low o'er the grass the swallow wings
> The cricket too how sharp he sings;
> Puss on the hearth with velvet paws
> Sits wiping o'er her whiskered jaws.
> Through the clear stream the fishes rise
> And nimbly catch the cautious flies.
> The glow worm, luminous and bright,
> illum'd the dewy dell last night.
> The frog has changed his yellow vest
> and in a russet coat is dressed.
> The whirling wind the dust obeys
> and then a rapid eddy plays;
> Though June, the air is cold and chill
> The mellow blackbirds voice is shrill;
> The dog so altered in his taste,
> quits mutton bones on grass to feast;

> See yon rooks how odd their flight,
> They imitate the gliding kite.
> And headlong downwards seem to fall
> as if they felt the piercing ball;
> It will surely rain, I see with sorrow
> Our jaunt must be put off tomorrow.

Much of the old traditional weather lore was in fact based on this poem. Thus, bad weather was on the way when the dog was seen eating grass or when soot was seen falling on the hearth or when the cat turned its back to the fire. If the cat began to scratch a tree this too indicated rain. When rain approached, the ducks began to quack more loudly about the farmyard while the hapless hens seemed listless and bedraggled. Having spent my childhood close to a rookery, I can still vividly recall some of the many times a storm was presaged from the erratic swerving and curving of the rooks on the wing. A congregation of starlings betokened frost.

Many lived near the coast and, in many coastal counties around the country, when seagulls or wild geese or other water birds strayed far inland this was taken as a sure sign that severe weather was on the way. A lone heron was not a good omen weatherwise. Yellow frogs indicated good weather, while brown frogs indicated bad weather. There was an old saying about the rainbow: 'A rainbow in the morning is the shepherd's warning; a rainbow at night is the shepherd's delight'.

Fine weather was presaged when smoke from the chimney rose straight up into the sky, when swallows flew low and when the western sky was red with the afterglow of the sinking sun. A robin carolling on top of a tree was another signal of good weather, but when the plover was heard at night, or when a flock of curlews rose to the east and flew to the west, then frosty weather was near at hand. There was an old saying that spring had finally arrived when the dusky brown form of the lark soared high in the sky. A wild pigeon crooning drowsily amongst the branches was taken as an omen of mild weather. In some parts it was believed that the cuckoo brought wild weather with it from foreign climes.

Bird Superstitions

The Robin and the Wren: A number of tales were told to explain how the robin acquired its distinctive red breast. The most popular of these was that which told of how, when Our Lord was hanging on the cross on Good Friday, the kindly robin came to him and plucked a thorn from the crown of thorns. A drop of the Saviour's precious blood fell onto the robin's breast which has remained that colour ever since, perhaps in recognition of the little bird's kindly deed. Thus the robin was blessed, and it was considered very unlucky to kill it or interfere with it in any way. Its practice of making its nest in peculiar places such as old kettles and troughs also endeared it to human kind.

If the robin was blessed then the wren was in many places an object of scorn. The reason for this was also pseudo-biblical:

At that time the soldiers were looking for Our Lord to kill him. He had to hide from them. One day he walked over a field where a man was sowing wheat, and drops of Our Saviour's blood fell on it, and by a miracle the wheat sprang up all in one night and was ready for reaping the next morning. On the next day the soldiers came by the same way in their search for Him. There was a robin in a bush in the wheat field and it saw the soldiers coming. It lay upon every drop of blood that marked Our Saviour's track and didn't leave a trace of it for the soldiers to follow, which is the reason that, from that day to this, the robin has a red breast. The captain of the soldiers asked the robin if it had seen a man passing that way lately.

'Not,' says the robin, 'since that wheat was sown.'

'At that rate,' says the captain of the soldiers, 'we are on the wrong track.' and he had his men turned round and was marching off with them when the wren came flying up and says:

'The wheat was sown yesterday; the wheat was sown yesterday.' And with that the soldiers were wheeled again, and away out the wheat field and never stopped till they came up with Our Saviour. And from that day the wren was cursed, and ever since it has been hunted and persecuted.

At one time all birds had the gift of speech but when the *deargán* (redpoll) betrayed Our Lord, that gift was taken from them. When the soldiers were looking for Christ the *deargán* gave the tidings of him saying, 'Nay, nay, Jesus crossed the field.'

There is another tradition which purports to explain the singular lack of popularity enjoyed by the diminutive wren. This time it was not Christ that the bird betrayed, but Saint Stephen. According to the story, when a crowd of men pursued the saint, the little bird flitted about the bushes in which Stephen had concealed himself, thus revealing his hiding place to his pursuers.

Yet another story was told, however, about the robin's acquisition of its beautiful red breast:

> Other people say that when there was only one fire long ago, a man and a boy were put to mind it in turns to keep it lighting. One day when the boy was minding the fire he fell asleep and a wolf came and quenched the fire. When he had the fire quenched he went away. Then a little robin came out of a bush near the fire and he saw that there was only one red spark left and he started clapping his wings until he lit the spark, and the flame grew bigger and bigger until at last it burned his breast. Some people say that this is how the robin got his red breast.

There is a lovely tale which describes the robin's association with the Irish missionary, St Columba:

> Long ago there lived a holy man named Columba. He lived in a house where he had a room to himself. One day as he was painting a book a robin redbreast hopped onto the window beside him.
>
> 'Will you sing me a song, birdie?' he asked. The robin began to sing and this is what he sang:
>
> > 'Holy, Holy, Holy, A wee brown bird am I.
> > But my breast is ruddy, Because I saw Christ die.'

Boys were told that if they robbed birds' nests they would get sore hands, and the robin's nest was the most inviolable of all. In some places, however, if a bird flew into the house – and robins were notorious for doing so in wintertime – then a death might be expected in the family. There was a contradictory tradition too which proclaimed that a bird flying into the house portended the birth of a baby. The robin has always been beloved of poets. Wordsworth asked, 'Art thou the bird

that man loves best/ The pious bird with the scarlet breast?'
Anthony Rye described how 'the redbreast smoulders in the
waste of snow', while the Irish poet, George Darley, lamented
the death of a robin: 'I strew thy bed who loved thy lays/ The
tear I shed, the cross I raise'.

Yet another reason was given to explain why the wren was
regarded with such antipathy. At one time a troop of Irish
soldiers was planning a surprise attack on the Cromwellian
army, but then a flock of wrens came and began to flap their
wings on the drums of the Irish, thus alerting their enemies
who rose up and made a great slaughter.

Of course for generations the wren was hunted throughout
Ireland in the days before Christmas. This was how the scene
was described by Mr and Mrs S. C. Hall in the 1840s:

> For some weeks preceding Christmas, crowds of village boys
> may be seen peering into hedges in search of the tiny wren; and
> when one is discovered the whole assemble and give eager
> chase to, until they have slain the little bird. In the hunt the
> utmost excitement prevails, shouting, screeching and rushing;
> all sorts of missiles are flung at the puny mark and not infre-
> quently they light upon the head of some less innocent being.
> From bush to bush, from hedge to hedge is the wren pursued
> and bagged with as much pride and pleasure as the cock of the
> woods by more ambitious sportsmen.

At first, the tourists were utterly at a loss to discover the reason
for this excitement and revelry until the enigma was finally
explained on the feast of St Stephen, 26 December:

> Attached to a huge holly bush, elevated on a pole, the bodies of
> several little wrens are borne aloft. This bush is an object of
> admiration in proportion to the number of dependent birds,
> and is carried through the streets in procession by a troop of
> boys, among whom may be usually found children of a larger
> growth, shouting and roaring as they proceed along and now
> and then stopping at some popular house and there singing the
> wren song. Of course contributions are levied in many quarters
> and the evening is, or rather was, occupied in drinking the sum
> total of the day's collection.

In some areas the tail feathers of robin or wren were substi-
tuted for the bird itself which prompted one commentator to
observe wryly that, 'in a severe winter a robin with a tail is
rarely seen.'

If contributions were not forthcoming from a particular

household, one of the wrens might be buried at the doorstep which was not only a great insult but also ensured that the hapless incumbents of the property enjoyed no great luck throughout the year that followed. There were a number of variations of the rhyme used on St Stephen's Day. Here is a particularly colourful one from Munster:

> The wren, the wren, the king of all birds
> St Stephen's Day was caught in the furze.
> Although he is little, his family was great
> Rise up landlady and give us a treat.
> And if this treat be very small
> sure it won't agree with the boys at all.
> And if this treat be of the best
> I hope in heaven your soul will rest.
> I followed my wren through frost and snow
> I followed my wren three miles or so.
> I followed my wren through Carraig an Ois,
> and brought her here on a holly bush.
> Here is the wren which ye can see
> Dressed high upon my holly tree.
> *Dreoilín, dreoilín*, where is your nest?
> It's in the woods where I love best.
> It's between the holly and the ivy tree
> where all the birds can whistle to me.
> I brought the wren to visit you here
> A happy Christmas and a merry New Year.
> Christmas comes but once a year
> And when it comes it brings good cheer.
> Up with the kettle and down with the pan
> A penny or two to bury the wran.

In some parts of the country it was neither Christ nor Stephen, nor indeed the troop of Irish soldiers, that the wren betrayed but Fionn Mac Cumhaill. When Fionn's pursuers drew near, the wren pinched his ear with her beak and his presence was revealed. According to this folktale, the little nip was visible on the hero's ear until the time of his death.

The wren is one of the most widely distributed resident birds in Ireland. It is the vertical tilt of the tail which gives the little wren its perky appearance. An old nursery rhyme tells how when the wren fell sick, the robin brought her food and wine but when the wren got better, she was less than grateful:

> Robin being angry hopped upon a twig
> Saying 'Out upon you! Fie upon you! Bold faced jig!'

One widespread and popular folktale centred on the robin and the advice it proffered to the widow's son:

There was once a widow who owned a small farm. She had three sons and each of the sons had a horse and a greyhound. One day the eldest son declared that he intended setting out to seek his fortune and he asked his mother to bake a cake of bread for him. When his mother was preparing the dough she asked her son which would he prefer: a big cake and her curse or a small cake and her blessing. The son replied: 'The biggest one you can make and your curse.' A short time afterwards, he took his horse and his greyhound and his fine big cake and went on his way.

After he had travelled some considerable distance, the eldest son sat down near a well to eat some of his cake and to give some to his dog. A robin came and asked for a tiny crumb of bread but the wanderer dourly told the little bird to be off with herself and to leave him in peace. Some time later, he encountered a hare, and his dog pursued the hare all day. At night he chanced upon a thatched cabin in the middle of a wood. Within was an old woman, her face lean and sickly in the flickering yellow lamplight. She pulled a 'rib of snare' from the horse's mane and told the newcomer to tie the dog and the horse with it. When this had been done, the old hag, who was really a witch, killed the eldest son through enchantment.

It was not many days later when the second son set out to seek his fortune too, having taken with him the big cake of bread and his mother's curse. The robin came to him too as he sat by the well but he was niggardly as his older brother and he would not spare even a crumb for the tiny little bird. He then encountered the hare and the witch and soon met the same fate as his older brother.

At length, the third son, the youngest, prepared to set forth in the hope of meeting his brothers again. When asked which cake he preferred, he chose the small cake and his mother's blessings. When he came to the well and when the robin asked for some bread he told her that she was welcome to eat all she could. The robin thanked him for his kindness and told him that he would soon meet a hare which was really a witch. The old hag owned a cabin in the woods and when she presented him with a 'rib of snare', asking him to tie his horse and his dog, he should throw it in the fire and burn it. He would then have the power to shoot the witch. When this had been done, said the robin, he must travel on until he came to a fabulous garden where he would see a beautiful princess. The garden contained three wonderful treasures: a singing bird, a talking tree and a flowing bowl. The princess would consent to marry him, and on the return journey he must spill three drops from the bowl onto each of the graves in the witch's yard. Then his brothers, their dogs and their horses would be well again. The flowing bowl was an enchanted bowl for it could never be emptied. The robin gave him her blessing and bade him goodbye.

Soon his dog startled the hare, and the hunt ended in the witch's cabin, but when the witch handed the rib of snare to the newcomer, he took it from her and secretly tossed it in the fire. It made a loud crackling sound and the youngest son observed that the hag's leg was bleeding, for his dog had snapped at the leg of the hare during the course of the chase. The young man took his gun and shot her, and promptly set out for the magical garden where he met the beautiful princess. They were soon married as the robin had predicted and, on his way back to his old home with his new bride, the youngest son spilled three drops from the enchanted bowl onto the graves near the witch's cabin. His brothers and their animals lived again, and there was great rejoicing. The youngest son and the princess invited his mother to come and live with them in the palace that overlooked the enchanted garden, and they all lived happily ever after.

If a robin perched directly in front of someone, that person might expect some important news or some important letter. The wren figured in a number of old sayings such as this optimistic one: 'Never despair while there's meat on the shin of a wren', and another which advised caution: 'Kill a wren but beware of fire.'

The wren builds a beautifully domed nest, which it lines with leaves or moss or bracken. The tiny white eggs display faint dark markings. According to Irish folklore tradition, the wren learned its nest building skills from the magpie which also enhances its nest with a roof of open work foliage.

* * *

The Crow Family: The raven is a member of the crow family and is often confused with the rook. It figures in old sayings such as 'The Raven's Curse on you' and 'The Raven thinks her own brood is white.' Its name in Irish is *Fiach Dubh* while the rook is known by the musical title of *Rucach*.

If one saw rooks looking down a chimney it was believed that someone would die in that house in the not too distant future. There must have been many ominous predictions then because, for some reason best known to themselves, rooks like nothing better than allowing the smoke from chimney pots to flow through their feathers. The term used by the experts is 'smoke bathing'. There was a very old tradition that the rook – sometimes the raven – had three drops of the devil's blood in it. On the other hand, it was considered very unlucky to hunt rooks out of a rookery. Rooks are admittedly not very colourful birds but they are surely as intrinsic a part of the Irish countryside as their more gaudy neighbours. If there were no rooks, generations of children would have been deprived of the pleasure of making a scarecrow. While rooks generally nest high in trees, one or two eccentric pairs have been known to nest on the ground.

Sir William Wilde wrote thus of another tradition related to the raven, as distinct from the rook:

> Among the many popular superstitions attendant upon the breeding and rearing of game fowl, it was believed that if an egg was extracted from a hawk or raven's or hooded crow's nest and a game egg placed therein, that nothing could beat the bird so-reared – that it always partook of the carnivorous propensity and indomitable courage of its nurse and the foster family with which it had been brought up.

Another tradition relates that when the Christ Child was born in Bethlehem, the raven was the first bird to fly low across the heavens, bringing the good news of the nativity to mankind.

There are several traditions in Irish folklore which describe the interference of birds in the siting or resiting of some important religious foundation. According to one story, St Brendan's Cathedral in Ardfert was originally to be built in a field called the Gallan Field. Construction began but the very first night a large flock of rooks removed the stones and the mortar to the west of Ardfert village where the church was then built, and where its ruins remain to this day.

The farmer's relationship with the rook has never been good. Yet, although the rook is known to damage greens and crops, he also eats harmful grubs and insects. Rooks are likeable, gregarious birds and it was never believed of them that they attacked new-born lambs in springtime, as did their near relative, the scaldcrow. There was an old rhyme which went:

> '"Caw, Caw," says the crow as he flies overhead,
> " 'tis time little Mary was going to bed."'

'The magpie' was the answer to the riddle which went: 'It is black; it is white; it hops on the road like hailstones'.

The magpie, or *snag breac*, was never very popular because it was said to steal eggs, sucking the goodness from the shells. The number of magpies you chanced to see presaged your luck for some time to come.

There was a trick question which asked: 'If you saw two magpies with one eye closed, how many magpies would you see with both eyes open?

To meet a lone magpie in the morning when one was setting out on a journey was considered a particularly bad omen, while if one chanced to see four magpies in a row this was a certain sign that some relative had died.

The magpie is an excellent nest builder, but one time when he very kindly offered to teach the tricks of the trade to the other birds all the other birds, save the wren, flew away in disgust, saying they knew perfectly well already how to build a nest. That is why the magpie and the wren build the best of nests.

The jackdaw is a small crow with a mischievous appearance. It takes great delight in building its nest in chimneys. It was seen as the collector in the world of birds, and those who had a tendency to hoard patently useless things were held to be as bad as the jackdaws.

The hooded crow has a number of names in Ireland since it is also known as the grey crow or the scald crow:

> Long ago a fox and a scaldcrow met and they decided to carry the fish from a little man by the name of Darby O'Drive from Bearna Beag. On Thursday evening as the little man came home, the fox lay across the road and pretended to be dead. The little man had just been asked for a fox's skin and he was delighted to get the fox. He threw him in the car near the basket of fish and then drove on.
>
> Then the fox had his chance. He put his head into the basket and threw the fish out one by one. Then the scaldcrow picked them up quickly and put them on the *gabhlóg* [v-shaped section] of an oak tree. This continued until nearly all the fish were out. On one occasion the little man turned round and saw the fox throwing out a fish. The fox knew he was seen and jumped quickly out of the car. Then he ran quickly to where the scaldcrow had the fish. On landing, the scaldcrow told him that he wouldn't get any fish so he thought of a plan. He asked the

scaldcrow for the herring at the bottom and she foolishly consented. When she pulled the foundation from the fish, they all fell down and the fox started laughing. The scaldcrow was so mad that she dashed to the fox but he quickly devoured her saying: 'I'd rather a fowl than a fish'.

If it was unlucky to interfere with a bird's nest it was courting disaster to interfere with a bird's nest in a fort. One day an audacious little boy set about robbing a crow's nest in the middle of a fort. The branch broke beneath him and he came crashing to the earth. He was not seriously hurt but badly shaken and so was promptly ordered to bed by his anxious mother. Next morning when he awoke his mouth had turned and remained so ever afterwards.

Another interesting story was told of a beautiful apple tree which grew in a fort. One day one of the local women was tempted to pick some of the apples. On her way home, all the crows began to fly about her. She threw an apple at them and they carried it off; she threw a second and a third, and so on until at length the crows had taken them all, but the crows were not crows at all for they were really the fairies.

* * *

Migrant Birds: Cuckoo, Corncrake and Swallow: As a child I was often told by the older people that I would have luck all summer long if I first heard the cuckoo with my right ear. Conversely, those who heard the cuckoo for the first time with their left ear would have bad luck. This was a widespread superstition right throughout the country. If you were stooping when you heard the cuckoo for the first time in the summer this presaged a death in the family; a death was also presaged if you heard the cuckoo in a graveyard.

When you heard the cuckoo for the first time, you should take note of where you were standing because it was there you would spend your life. Also, you should take off your shoe or boot, and if you found a hair in it, you would marry a person with hair of the same colour. It was believed in some parts that when the cuckoo was flying to Ireland, it brought a bit of a stick on its back and, when it felt tired, it placed the stick beneath its breast and floated on it. The cuckoo's flight pattern does in fact incorporate rapid beating of the wings and glides.

What could be more lovely than to hear the song of the cuckoo on a sultry summer's day? Nevertheless, oats which had not been sown before 1 April were derided as being 'cuckoo oats'.

It was considered very unlucky to kill the cuckoo or to break its eggs because the cuckoo brought fine weather with her, though in some parts she was seen as the harbinger of wild weather!

One colourful tradition links the cuckoo with St John:

> It is said that the cuckoo is heard no more after the 29th June because the day before St John was martyred the cuckoo was cooing all day long and in the evening St John said: 'Shut up. We are bothered from you.' After that the cuckoo was never heard from the 29th June onwards.

The older cuckoos, the parent birds, were believed to migrate from Ireland in the early days of August while the younger birds generally lingered on until the end of September.

The corncrake boasts beautiful chestnut wings which are very distinctive when the bird is in flight. There were throughout the country a number of traditions about this shy and elusive visitor. For instance, in some parts it was firmly believed that the corncrake made its familiar *crek-crek* sound by lying on its back on the ground and rubbing its legs together. However, my own favourite tradition about the corncrake was that it changed, through some mysterious metamorphosis, into a water hen, or *cearc uisce*, during the winter months.

It was considered very unlucky to bring a corncrake, alive or dead, into the house. If, however, you wished bad luck on someone, you might say: *'Nar fheice tú an chuach na an traonach arís!'* (That you may not live to see cuckoo or corncrake again!)

The chorus of twittering swallows is one of the magical sounds of summer, while their graceful sweeping in and out of sheds is a joy to remember when cold winter draws near again. The old saying asserts that one swallow never made a summer. It was bordering on the sacrilegious to interfere with the swallow or with its nest, for if this were done the cows would milk blood. Likewise, when someone had their hair cut, the clippings were never left lying about, for if the swallows found them and used them in their nest, the one whose hair had been taken would be prone to headaches all summer long. If, on the other hand, a swallow flew into the dwelling house, this was considered to be a very good omen.

* * *

The Blackbird and the Thrush: The blackbird with its striking orange bill is one of the most familiar and melodious birds of the Irish countryside, the notes of his song rich and fluted. The whistle of the blackbird, however, indicated that rain was on the way, and the blackbird was not well liked in parts, for it made clandestine raids on fruit bushes and sometimes scratched thatch from roofs.

There was an old saying which asserted that there would be white blackbirds before an unwilling woman tied the knot.

I often heard about the hunting or torching of blackbirds and thrushes which was a common practice throughout the countryside, but there were salutary tales told of misadventure on such occasions:

> John Lyons, Ballyhorgan, Lixnaw, went one night torching up Gentleman's Avenue, Ballyhorgan. The place was supposed to be haunted. John Lyons killed a few birds and was about to kill a thrush when the latter spoke *'Ná buail! Ná buail!'* cried the thrush. At the same time, a cold hand slapped his face and the torch was flung from his hand. He was an invalid for three months but was never in better of the shock.

The birds were killed not for sport or pleasure but for food, for blackbird and thrush were cooked and eaten when meat was scarce.

When winter came, boys and girls made cribs for catching birds especially those such as the blackbird and the thrush which wandered into the farmyard in frost and snow. The crib was made of elder twigs fastened by light slender sticks at one end. At the other end was a light twig in the form of a bow which served as a trap door. The front end of the crib was raised from the ground. The bird was lured inside by pieces of bread, grains of oats or chopped fat. When it hopped on the light twig the crib fell, and the hapless bird was a prisoner. Most birds were released in a matter of seconds.

One old proverb proclaimed that the three most wholesome foods for the drover were the back of a herring, the belly of a salmon and the head of a thrush. Thomas Hardy wrote a lovely poem called 'The Darkling Thrush', but here is a tale in a lighter vein:

> One day as Thomas Aherne was going from Knockanure to Listowel he saw a thrush on the roadside. He heard the thrush singing and he understood what the bird was saying: This is

what she said: 'Spend and God will send'. He had a pound but when he was coming home he only had three half pence. The thrush was in the same place and this is what she said this time: 'Have it yourself or be without it'.

* * *

Geese, Swans and Ducks: During the Middle Ages – as, indeed, in much later times – it was forbidden in Ireland to eat meat during Lent. Yet it was allowable to eat the flesh of the barnacle goose for a popular Irish belief asserted that the birds were really a kind of fish, and were born on timber at the bottom of the sea. Giraldus Cambrensis, who had a vivid imagination at the best of times, wrote in *Topographica Hibernica* in 1186:

> They are produced from timber tossed along the sea and are at first like gum. Afterwards they hang down by their beaks as if they were seaweed attached to the timber and are surrounded by shells in order to grow more freely. Having thus in the process of time been clothed with a strong coat of feathers, they either fall into the water or fly freely away into the air. They derive their food and growth from the sap of the wood or from the sea by a secret and most wonderful process of alimentation. I have frequently seen with my own eyes more than a thousand of these small birds hanging down on the sea shore from one piece of timber enclosed in their shells and already formed. They do not breed and lay eggs like other birds nor do they ever hatch any eggs, nor do they seem to build nests in any corner of the earth. Hence bishops and religious men in some parts of Ireland do not scruple to dine off those birds at the time of fasting because they are not flesh nor born of flesh.

One colourful old saying reminds us that a wild goose never reared a tame gosling.

It was considered very unlucky to kill a swan, and salutary tales were told of the dire consequences that befell those who did so. Farm animals often died mysteriously soon afterwards.

'Fian fian' was the phrase used to call the ducks. There were many people in the countryside who preferred ducks' eggs to hens' eggs, and so the duck was a familiar sight in farmyards too. Here is a funny story about ducks:

> A certain man who lives in the townland of Moynsha hired a servant boy at the market in Abbeyfeale. He was a good servant in every way but was lazy getting up in the mornings. The

farmer had a flock of ducks which were never put in a house. They slept in the yard in front of the house every night. Every morning when calling the boy to get up the farmer said, 'Get up, Jack, don't you hear the ducks saying, "Day, day, day".' This occurred nearly every morning. When Christmas Eve came the boy called the master very early in the morning:

   'Get up, sir,' said he, 'don't you hear the ducks saying, "Pay, pay, pay".'

There are many species of wild duck in Ireland, the best known and the best loved being the mallard. The mallard is, in fact, the ancestor of most farmyard varieties of duck. When alarmed, mallards rise with rapid noisy wing beats and loud quacks. The drake has a lustrous green head, white neck ring and curled black upper-tail feathers.

The geese were called with the words 'Baddy, baddy, baddy', and *fómhar na ngéanna* occurred on St Michael's Day, 29 September, when a fat and flavoursome goose provided a succulent centre piece for steaming hot potatoes and vegetables.

Great flocks of geese that had been hatched in the springtime were a common sight in the countryside where they cackled noisily in laneways and farmyards. Many of the geese were taken to the market at Michaelmas and it was customary in many places to stuff mattresses and pillows with the down which had been plucked from the birds. In some parts, however, a lamb was killed instead of a goose, perhaps in honour of the tradition that St Michael restored to life one of the sons of the High King of Ireland, whereupon, in gratitude, the boy's mother, the queen, vowed that she would annually at Michaelmas bestow on the poor, one sheep of every flock she possessed in memory of the saint's wonderful kindness to her.

One of Samuel Lover's best loved tales was that of King O'Toole and the Goose. The king in his youth loved riding and hunting, but when he grew old and stiff in his limbs he chose a goose as his constant companion. 'And the way the goose divarted him was this way; you see the goose used for to swim across the lake and go down for throut (and no finer throut in all Ireland than the same throut) and cotch fish on a Friday for the king and flew every other day round about the lake divartin' the poor king, the way you'd think he'd break his sides laughin' at the frolicksome tricks av his goose; so in coorse of time the goose was the biggest pet in the country and the biggest rogue and the poor king was as happy as the day was long.' Then one day the goose too had grown old and had been stricken with the same disease as his master, the king, who was sorely grieved at the plight of his faithful companion. Not long afterwards the king encountered St Kevin who offered to make the much-loved goose as good as new if the King granted him as a reward all the lands flown over by the goose on her first flight following her restoration to good health. The king agreed, whereupon the saint blessed the goose, marking her with the Sign of the Cross. 'With that she took to her heels, flying like wan o' the aigles themselves, and cuttin' as many capers as a swallow before a shower of rain'. The goose flew over a great sweep of land before returning to land at her master's feet. The King was as good as his word, and that was the way so much land came into the possession of St Kevin all at once, 'For the goose flewn round every individual acre o' King O'Toole's property you see, being let into the saycret by St Kevin who was mighty cute. Meanwhile the king had his goose as good as new to "divart him" as long as he lived.' However, not long afterwards the goose met an untimely end, for one day when she went fishing for trout she was killed by an eel. 'Howsummdever, the king never recovered the loss iv his goose, though he had her stuffed (I don't mane stuffed with praties and inyans but as a curiosity) and preserved in a glass case for his own divarshin and the poor king died on the next Michaelmas day which was remarkable.'

There were a number of old sayings about the goose and the gander. Here are some, variations on a theme, which cautioned against stupidity: 'Don't send the goose with a message to the fox's den', 'Don't put the fox minding the geese', and 'When the fox is the preacher let the goose not listen to his sermon'. Another proverb advised patience: 'Small goslings make fine geese'.

The wings of dead geese and turkeys were often adapted by imaginative housewives and served as colourful dusters. Apparently these novel dusters were quite efficient, but then those were simple times – there were no ozone destructive polishes then, and certainly no disposable towels.

The following story was told about Daniel O'Connell and the Goose:

Daniel O'Connell was a very wealthy man and he had many servants. One day he was travelling home from some place with one of these servants and they saw a flock of geese on the road. One of the geese stood on one leg with the other leg raised up beneath her breast. Anyone who saw her would swear she had only one leg. They continued on until they reached home where a fine meal had been prepared for the Liberator with a roast goose in the centre of the table. When the servant girl found O'Connell's back turned for a moment, she grabbed one of the legs from the roast goose. He asked the servant girl when and where she had procured that goose. 'Oh', said the girl, 'That's the goose we saw on the road.'

Interference with the body of a dead swan was something to be avoided:

One time there lived an old man near Killorglin. His wife was dead. He had a lot of money and did not know where to hide it. One day he was walking along the bank of the river Laune and he saw a swan dead, as he thought. He picked her up and saw an empty space inside in her. He thought he would put his treasure into her and bury her in the garden. He did so and after one day the swan rose out of the earth and flew away with his money. The old man got so angry that he died. Ever since the swan comes to visit the place where she was buried in the garden.

* * *

The Eagle: One of the most remarkable views in the environs of Killarney is that of the majestic mountain, the Eagle's Nest which was so evocatively depicted on canvas by the artist, Jonathan Fisher, and which no self-respecting Victorian tourist would deign to visit without having the bugle played or the cannon fired for the benefit of creating the startling echoes. One visitor, Arthur Wakefield, recorded that the explosion of the cannon, multiplied by the chasms in the rugged cliffs all around, seemed to roll majestically round the hills till, after many repetitions, the sound gradually sank into gentle murmurs at a distance.

One of the most fascinating birds in the area was the golden eagle, *aquila chrysateos*. During the breeding season, the birds could be seen wheeling and reeling above the eyrie in the Eagle's Nest. According to tradition, one eagle had reached the venerable old age of a thousand years, having for generations been seen to haunt the far-famed lakes.

The practice of taking birds and eggs from the nest continued throughout much of the nineteenth century. The rocks where the nests were built were so steep that they could only be reached with ropes from above. As the Killarney Eagle was a particularly shy bird, such activities as well as the persistent intrusion of visitors, the thunder of the cannon, and the attacks on the species by sheep farmers caused a sharp reduction in the numbers about the lakes. The magnificent bird, with its wing span of $6^{1}/_{2}$–$7^{1}/_{2}$ feet, was so rare by the 1870s that considerable excitement was aroused when a pair of golden eagles built their nest on top of the Eagle's Nest. By 1900 however the species was extinct in Ireland.

A favourite Victorian legend about the Eagle's Nest had as its central character a soldier who, indeed, regularly played the part of the villain in legends of Killarney: Apparently the soldier determined to steal the young birds from the nest on the mountain. So, as soon as the mother bird had flown away, he let himself down by a rope from the top of the cliff. However, the old eagle returned unexpectedly and asked the newcomer to explain the reason for his visit. The soldier, 'a little bit frightened at the sight of the bright eyes with the hooked bake between 'um' replied that he had come only to pay his respects to the eagle family. Not convinced by this flimsy excuse the eagle thought of a plan to discover the truth. The story went on:

'I'll just make bold to ax a neighbour of mine that lives in the rock here. Hello there, Mistress Echo, did this fellow come to rob the Eagle's Nest?'

'To rob the Eagles Nest. To rob the Eagles Nest,' says Mistress Echo.

'There now do you hear that?' says the eagle but the soldier without waiting to answer began to climb up the rope as fast as he could.

'Not so fast, Mr Soldier,' says the eagle. 'Not so fast, my fine fellow. As you came to pay me a visit, 'tis only fair I should show you the shortest way home.'

So with that she gave him a clink over the head with wan of her wings and then with a kick of her claw sent him down into the river in a jiffy. It was well for him it was into the river he fell or surely he'd be smashed to bits.

Here is another tale, this time about the fox and the eagle, recorded in 1945 from a storyteller in Caherdaniel, Co Kerry:

It was a very lean time. The hungry fox wandered about the shores of the Lakes of Killarney and he could find nothing to eat. Then he saw three fine ducks swimming on the water a little distance from the shore and he assured himself that if he could catch them, they would provide him with a very wholesome meal. There was a plant with very big leaves growing nearby and taking two of the biggest leaves he could find he used them to help him swim out towards the ducks. The misfortunate ducks did not know anything until the fox had carried off one of their number. He returned to the shore, deposited his fist victim and decided he would try and grab her companions too. He snatched the second duck and laid her beside the first but when he returned the third time he found that the brace of ducks he had left behind on the shore were nowhere to be seen. He was greatly perplexed. Who was playing tricks on him? He looked up and seeing the eagles nest high on the mountain he concluded that there lived his culprit, but how to get his revenge. That was the question. Then he noticed a fire smouldering in the distance and taking the third duck he dragged her backwards and forwards through the embers. Then he laid the duck on the shore and concealed himself in a clump of bushes. The eagle swooped down and snatched the duck but the feathers of the duck had been reddened by the fire. The unsuspecting eagle deposited her prize in the nest, whereupon the nest caught fire and was ablaze in a matter of seconds. The burning nest tumbled down the mountain side and the fox had not only three ducks for his supper but three dead eaglets for his larder.

Shaun Mór who lived on the island of Inis Shark had a strange encounter with an eagle and other creatures:

There was an old man on the island called Shaun Mór who said that he had often travelled at night with the little men and carried their sacks for them; and in return they gave him strange fairy gifts and taught him the secret of power so that he could always triumph over his enemies; and even as to the fairies he was as wise as any of them and could fight half a dozen of them together if he were so minded and pitch them into the sea or strangle them with seaweed. So the fairies were angered at his pride and presumption and determined to do him a malicious turn, just to amuse themselves when they were up for fun. So one night when he was returning home he saw a great river between him and his house. 'How shall I get across now?' he cried aloud and immediately an eagle came up to him. 'Don't cry, Shaun Mór,' said the eagle 'but get on my back and I'll carry you safely.' So Shaun mounted and they flew right up ever so high, till at last the eagle tumbled him off by the side of a great mountain in a place he had never seen before.

'This is a bad turn you have played on me,' said Shaun. 'Tell me where I am now?' 'You are on the moon,' said the eagle, 'and get down the best way you can for now I must be off, so goodbye. Mind you don't fall off the edge. Goodbye.' So with that the eagle disappeared. Just then a cleft in the rock opened and out came a man as pale as the dead with a reaping hook in his hand. 'What brings you here?' said he 'Only the dead come here.' And he looked fixedly at Shaun Mór like one already dying.

'Oh your worship,' he said. 'I live far from here. Tell me how am I to get down and help me, I beseech you.'

'Aye that I will,' said the pale faced man. 'Here is the help I give you.' and with that he gave him a blow with the reaping hook which tumbled Shaun right over the edge of the moon and he fell ever and ever so far till luckily he came in the midst of a flock of geese and the old gander that was leading stopped and eyed him:

'What are you doing here, Shaun Mór?' said he. 'For I know you well. I've often seen you down in Shark. What will your wife say when she hears of your being out so late at night, wandering about in this way? It is very disreputable and no well brought up gander would do the like, much less a man. I am ashamed of you, Shaun Mór.'

'O, your honour,' said the poor man, 'it's an evil turn of the evil witches for they have done all this; but let me just get up on your back and if your honour brings me safe to my own house I shall be forever grateful to every goose and gander in the world for as long as I live.'

'Well then get up on my back,' said the bird, fluttering its wings with a great clatter over Shaun, but he couldn't manage at all to get on its back, so he caught hold of one leg and he and the gander went down and down till they came to the sea.

'Now let you go,' said the gander 'and find your way home the best way you can, for I have lost a great deal of time with you already and must be away.' And he shook off Shaun Mór who dropped plump down into the sea, and when he was almost dead a great whale came sailing by and flapped him all over with its fins. He knew no more till he opened his eyes lying on the grass in his own field by a great stone and his wife was standing over him drenching him with a great pale of water and flapping his face with her apron.

* * *

The Kingfisher: The kingfisher is one of Ireland's most colourful birds, but most views of the kingfisher are exceedingly brief – an electric flash of blue near some secluded stream. It feeds mainly on small fish which it catches by plunging through the water from an overhanging branch or from a tree stump or by skilfully hovering above the water before striking at its prey. The nest hole is generally excavated in a bank and slopes slightly upwards, the beautiful eggs being round and glossy white.

Writing in 1852 in his book entitled *Vacations in Ireland*, Christopher Weld noted the following tradition about the kingfisher:

> I was prepared to hear from my fishing attendant that this gaudy bird is regarded with considerable superstition by the Kerry peasants who suppose it to be endowed with marvellous attributes. Amongst these the belief yet exists that a kingfisher in full plumage is an antidote against certain diseases and when stuffed and suspended by a thread its bill points to the quarter from whence the wind blows.

* * *

The Plover: The grey plover is seen mainly in winter in Ireland as it is a passage migrant. Numbers are generally small but on occasion large flocks have been sighted. There was an old saying: 'It's a long way from home that the plover cries.' When the plover was heard at night or was seen standing quietly in a field this was taken as a sign of frost. The arrival of the grey plover in coastal areas was a sign that biting winds were on the way.

* * *

The Pigeon: A wild pigeon crooning in a tree was an indication of mild weather. It was believed that pigeons sometimes accompanied funerals to graveyards and it was held to be very unlucky if a pigeon flew into a farmyard where there were not pigeons already. Here is a colourful little tale which features the pigeon:

> Long ago there lived a man who had two children, a boy and a girl. Their mother died when they were young and their father married a second time. The wife had a daughter who was ugly. She hated her stepchildren and wanted to kill them. One day she went to a druid and the druid gave her an enchanted rod. When she came home she struck the boy with it and he was turned into a calf. Then she struck the girl and she was turned into a pigeon. She told their father that they were gone visiting. Not long after this, her daughter got sick and nothing would cure her but the liver and lights of the calf. The calf was to be killed one day when a butcher came. When he was going to stick the calf, the pigeon flew in and began to say: 'O brother, O brother, are you going to die? O brother, O brother, sorry am I.'

The butcher would not stick the calf. They could get no butcher to stick him. Next day he went at him the pigeon began the same thing. The man followed her. The pigeon flew into the room where the enchanted rod was. She rubbed herself to it and got her own shape back again. She took the rod and did the same thing to the calf and he got his own shape. The old woman and her daughter were killed.

* * *

The Curlew: The long legged curlew with its curved bill is one of our most familiar wading birds. Its nest is essentially a large saucer of grass in relatively open ground, while the beautiful pear shaped eggs are a glossy olive green etched with brown markings. The nest of the curlew is thus well camouflaged, which may account for one of the most popular traditions about the curlew in Ireland, that it built no nest at all.

There was an old story which associated the curlew with Our Lord:

They say that one day Our Lord went into a cave to rest and He fell asleep. After some time the Jews came along looking for Him. When they were near the cave in which Our Lord was, a curlew began to scream and the screaming woke Our Lord and He was able to escape. Our Lord then blessed the curlew and gave it the instinct to build its nest in a way that no man can find.

When the curlew produced a double whistle this was taken as a sign of approaching rain.

* * *

The Dove: In Irish folklore, the dove was associated with Noah and the Ark:

God warned Noah that he would send a great flood and so Noah built the Ark. He took in seven birds of each kind of bird into the ark. After some time, he sent out one of the birds to see if the flood waters had subsided but that bird never returned. He then chose the dove and he asked her to go out and see if the flood had receded. She did this and soon returned. There was nothing in her beak but Noah sent her forth again and when she came back to the ark the second time she brought with her an olive branch in her beak. This Noah interpreted as a signal that the tops of the trees were now uncovered and that the raging swell of the flood was subsiding at last. Thus the dove was deemed to be a very wise bird and ever since that time she has taken messages from one country to another all over the world.

* * *

The Heron: Cranes are not resident nor do they migrate here in large numbers. Thus, the stipulation that the body of a crane should be buried for a month in some suitable container in a manure heap, probably referred to the heron which is known in Irish as the *corr riasc*. At the end of the month a greasy oil should have collected in the bottom of the container and this oil was held to be a very effective cure for burns. The heron is an excellent fisherman and its silhouette in flight is very distinctive.

* * *

The Lark: There was an old saying 'as melodious as a lark'. If one heard a boastful person making extravagant plans for the future one might reply cynically: 'When the sky falls we'll all catch larks'. Yet another old saying stressed the importance of the innate nature of things: 'Every bird as she is reared and the lark for the bog'. If the lark was heard in the morning on St Brigid's day this would presage a sunny day, and those who heard it would enjoy good fortune throughout the year. The lark was said to be sacred to St Brigid for its song awoke her every morning to her prayers.

* * *

Other Birds: Sparrows hopping on the road were an indication of bad weather, while a congregation of starlings was taken as a sign of frost. It was believed that if a person with jaundice could fix his gaze on a yellowhammer, the patient would be cured but the bird would die, this being just one instance of disease transference in Irish folklore. At one time the oystercatcher could swim but the seagull deceived her and stole her swimming gear. The oystercatcher was said to be marked with a cross.

* * *

The Cock and the Hen: A white cock in the yard was said to be very lucky. However, if a cock crowed through the door or window of a house, this presaged a death in the family. A sop hanging from a hen's tail was a sign of a funeral, while a sop across her back implied that someone in the house would die in the near future and the coffin would be shouldered to the cemetery. These were just some of the many superstitions about the cock and the hen at a time when large flocks of hens were a familiar sight in farmyards throughout the country-side. 'God send us good luck', was what some people said when they heard the cock crow. 'God between us and all harm', was what they said when the cock crew at night.

When eggs were placed in a nest for hatching they might be sprinkled with holy water or marked with ashes from a branch or palm which had been blessed on Palm Sunday and which had been burned with a blessed candle. In some parts, when the eggs had hatched the woman of the house did not throw away the egg shells but ranged them along the walls of the cow house where they served as a kind of collective amulet to ward off evil spirits. Egg shells generally were held to be the dwelling place of fairies which was why they were always crushed when the egg was eaten.

There were a number of traditions which served to explain why hens were continually scratching the earth with their feet. One of the most popular related that when Our Lord was fleeing from his pursuers, He sought refuge in an underground cave. When the soldiers were on the point of passing over the cave, without the slightest indication that Christ was directly beneath them, they noticed the hens scratching the earth. They went towards them and the hens had already scratched away sufficient earth to reveal the entrance to the cave. The soldiers searched the cave and captured Our Lord. From that time onwards, it was said, the hen could not find a single bite to eat without first scratching the earth with her feet.

Hens very often did great damage in flower gardens and vegetable plots when they scratched the soil away from the precious plants; but some people apparently had a novel plan to deal with this perennial problem:

> They went to the strand and picked barnacles, boiled them and took out the fish. Then they took out the bottom of the shell and put the shell on the hens' feet and every time the hens began to scratch the shells hurt them and prevented them from doing so. This custom was found valuable but only those near the sea could avail of it.

Here is one of my favourite folktales about hens:

> In this parish there is a townland called Gortdromagauna and

years ago when motor cars were very seldom seen, the people near the road would stand to see every car that came the way. One day an old man who lived near the road was crossing the road. He had a lot of hens and some of them followed him and they were picking around when a motor car drove by and killed eight of them. The driver stopped the car and came back to see the amount of damage he had done. The old man told him that he had killed eight of them. The driver offered him two shillings a piece for them. The old man was delighted and asked the driver if he would be passing that way again. The driver wondered why he asked that question. The old man answered: 'So that I can have all my hens on the road the next time you pass.'

There were many old sayings about the hen, one of the most popular being 'A whistling woman and a crowing hen. There is no luck in the house they're in.' Another warned against the temptations of avarice: 'Eating and complaining like the greedy hen'. It was also said that it was a bad bird that dirtied her own nest and a bad bird that wouldn't scratch herself. The notion that wisdom comes with old age was encapsulated in the saying: 'The old bird is not caught with chaff', while caution was advised in the proverb: 'Don't count your chickens before they are hatched'. Curses were fairly common place too and a well-liked example was 'Six eggs to you and a half a dozen of them rotten'. Indeed, one of the best ways of bringing bad luck on one's neighbour was by burying rotten eggs on his property. If, however, you had the misfortune to find eggs thus buried, the antidote for the curse was to toss the eggs behind the fire and allow them to burn slowly. The black hen was smarter than the white hen. Why? The black hen could lay a white egg but the white hen couldn't lay a black egg. There were many old sayings too which referred to the farmyard cock. One of the most popular cautioned against vanity: 'Every cock crows on his own dunghill'. If the cock crew at unusual times, especially at night, then the death of a relative or family member had occurred or would occur in the very near future. However, when the cock crew in the morning the people of the *sídhe* ceased their wanderings and returned to their forts and their fairy mounds. It was considered advisable to postpone a journey if you encountered a crowing cock a little distance from the door.

The feet of the cock had certain curative properties if one accepts the veracity of the following tale:

Years ago in Bonane there lived an old woman called *an bean feasa* who used to go around with the fairies. In one house lived a child of four years old who was unable to walk. It was the custom at that time to keep the hens in a coop in the kitchen. The old woman came to see the child and told them that the cure was in the kitchen. They asked her of its whereabouts and she said 'In that old gentleman, there,' pointing to the cock. 'Take him out and wash his feet three nights in water and wash the child's feet each night in the same water afterwards.' They did as she told them and the child walked and was all right.

There is also in Irish folklore a quasi-biblical tale concerning the cock. The cock was boiling in a pot over a fire and a group of non-believers were discussing the Crucifixion of Christ, as they stood about the fire. 'We have buried Christ now,' they said, 'and he has no more power to rise from the dead than the cock that is cooking in this pot.' Immediately the cock leapt onto the rim of the pot and crowed twelve times saying '*Mac na-h-Óighe Slán*' (The Virgin's Son is saved). From that time onwards it was the custom for some old women to say '*Mac na h-Óighe Slán*' each time the cock crew.

Long ago many people kept a march cock as they thought such a cock would keep away the fairies. The cock also figured in a curse. '*Ide coileach Eamonn ort*' (The curse of Eamonn's cock on you). This was based on the sad tale of the vain cock who studied his reflection for so long in a well that he eventually fell into the well and drowned.

The fox is generally portrayed as a crafty animal but in one folktale which was popular right throughout the country the cock outwitted the fox:

Once upon a time the fox snatched a cock from the hen house. A fine fat cock he was that would fill the pot. When he came to the door of his den, the fox laid down the cock to kill him. He took a firm grip about the nape of the cock's neck and pressed his two front legs down upon the cock's back so that the poor unfortunate cock was in a bad way. The fox was just about to bite off his victim's head when the cock spoke.

'Now, Mr Fox,' he said. 'You should be grateful to God that you have me to eat and you should give thanks to Him from the bottom of your heart before you set about eating me.'

'That was a wholesome and holy thought indeed,' said the fox. It was well for those who knew how to give thanks but he himself did not know how to do so.

'Let not that be your excuse from this time onwards,' said the cock. 'I will be happy to teach you if you wish.'

'I would think it a great kindness if you would,' said the unsuspecting fox.

'Very well, clasp your two front paws together like this – look!' said the cock, demonstrating the correct method to the fox. 'And lift your eyes to heaven.'

He loosened his grasp on the cock, then clasped his two front paws together and averted his gaze towards heaven. No sooner had he done so than off with the cock at the rate of a mile a minute. When the fox had looked up for a very long time and had heard nothing further from his instructor he turned round but the cock was nowhere to be seen. 'My thousand curses on any one who gives thanks for his food before he has it inside his belly,' he cried in frustration for he knew that he had been outwitted by the wily cock.

A cock was often killed on St Martin's Day and the blood spattered on the door. Some of the blood was also spilled on a white cloth which might then be used to stop bleeding in humans as well as animals.

'Tuk tuk' was the expression used to call the hens, while the woman of the house called out 'Bee, bee, bee' when she wanted the turkeys to come to her. Turkeys very often represented an additional source of income when they were sold at the fair in the days before Christmas, which was why one amusing old saying proclaimed that a turkey never voted for Christmas.

* * *

Cures for Poultry: There were several cures for the pip in poultry. This was caused by an infection in the throat. One remedy was to blow tobacco smoke down the bird's throat since it was believed that the smoke would kill the infection. Alternatively, a few drops of turpentine might be allowed to fall down the throat from the end of a quill. Sometimes the bird might be placed in a bag which had been well dusted with lime. The bag was then shaken vigorously and the lime-dust killed the infection in the throat. Another cure was to place the bird in a bag which contained a saucer of oil and to leave her there for two or three days. One might also place a rib of horse hair down the throat.

Dandelions and nettles boiled and mixed with gruel helped to improve the condition of young birds. If a turkey had cramps in her leg, the leg was placed into a rotten potato for nine mornings and nine nights in succession.

Animal Superstitions

The Stoat: There are no weasels in Ireland but the stoat has long been referred to in country places as the weasel. The Irish stoat is an endemic species and is generally smaller and darker than its British counterpart. The reddish brown fur of the stoat may whiten or partially whiten in wintertime. Large numbers of stoats have sometimes been seen together. A pack of stoats made an attack on a woman and her dog in Burtonport, County Donegal in the 1960s. The woman fled but the dog was killed. This, however, was very much an isolated incident and the stoat, though a fierce little fellow, does not generally interfere with humankind unless provoked.

The tendency of stoats to form packs from time to time may be responsible for the widespread folk belief that weasels from the surrounding countryside all came together for the funeral of a relative. Two of the chief mourners carried the corpse, each of them holding between its teeth one end of the body of the deceased, with the remaining mourners forming an orderly procession behind them. There was another widespread tradition that, in times of crisis, the weasel summoned his fellows to his side by placing the tip of his tail between his teeth and whistling.

Very often the female might be referred to as 'the lady' or 'the noble lady', the *bean uasal*. One of the most popular of all beliefs about the weasel was that there was poison in its spittle.

There are several versions from round the country of the story, describing the weasels' encounter with the haymakers. The following comes from County Limerick:

One of the older women used to tell how on one occasion while mowing a large meadow, the men found a nest of young weasels, which they saved and placed in a tuft of hay in a bush. One of the mowers, a short time afterwards, looked back and saw two grown weasels putting something green into the tin of milk for the men's drink. He told his fellows who watched and saw the animals search and find their young which they put in a place of safety, after which they returned and with some difficulty upset the poisoned milk.*

This variation on the same theme comes from County Clare:

> Mrs O'Callaghan was told by a mower there that he killed a young weasel in the grass and his wife saw the old ones spit in his sour milk. She wanted to throw it away but he would not believe her. A short time afterwards he got violent gripes and gave himself up for lost, the doctor having much difficulty to get him to take any remedy.*

Yet another Limerick tale records how a youth named Butler killed a nest of weasels and was pursued 'for miles by the irate parents up onto the table of a farmer who sat at dinner, and who with his sons had some difficulty in killing with their knives the revengeful little beasts, which entirely confined their attacks to the culprit.'

Here is yet another story of weasel vengeance:

> It was said that the weasel was very clever and he exacts vengeance for any wrong done to him. One time a stook of oats was knocked and the people found what they thought was a nest of rats. They killed every one of the young. Then the parents came out and they knew they were weasels. The people of the house had two clutches of goslings and they were inside in a shed during the course of the night. Next morning every single gosling was stretched dead by the weasel.*

The story of the weasels who spilled the can of poisonous milk portrays the animal as a creature grateful to humans for the kindness that had been shown their young. Similarly, there were many folktales of animals fetching remedies for humans who had helped them in some way. The remedy very often consisted of magical healing herbs and leaves and they were often brought by the wily weasel.

The weasel was in many ways admired for its courage. While a purse made of its skin was thought to bestow great good fortune on its owner – 'In my boyish days a stoatskin or as they were nearly universally called in Ireland a weasel skin purse was considered lucky while a piebald weasel skin purse was the height of good luck' – on the other hand it was held to be extremely unlucky to kill a weasel deliberately, for it would not be long before the relatives of the deceased would descend with great savagery on the house of the murderer. One might spare oneself some of the more dire consequences, however, if one immediately sacrificed a hen, said a few prayers over the body and suspended it from a post in the yard.

---

*From *Journal of the Royal Society of Antiquaries*, 1896.

It was said that anywhere a weasel could put through his head he could also put through his body, and in many parts of the country weasels, or more correctly stoats were valued as killers of rats.

* * *

The Badger: Man's relationship with the badger has never been a happy one. One bloodthirsty eighteenth-century Irish commentator observed that the best use that could be made of a badger was 'to kill him with hounds or mastiffs, or if you have young terriers that would enter, the best is to cope or muzzle him so that he cannot bite and put him into an earth.'

The badger has long had a bad press and is often blamed for crimes for which he is not responsible. Only very rarely does he raid the hen house or kill a lamb. He has been linked, some would say unjustifiably, with the spread of bovine TB. The writer of a booklet published in 1967 did something to redress the balance when he wrote that the average badger was an asset to the countryside and should be left in peace. The badger was generally left undisturbed in potato fields anyway, for while it was held that he liked to eat weeds, he had no taste for potato stalks.

William Thompson was one of the first to outline in some detail the theory that there are in fact two types of badger – the dog badger, a carnivore and the pig badger, largely herbivore. This belief had a special place in Irish folk tradition. It was also widely believed in Ireland that the badgers were descendants of the pigs which the Vikings had brought with them into the country. They were held to be extremely clever animals who never took poison. They were believed to eat roots which they found in marshes and bogs and which they extracted from the soil with their sharp claws. In many areas of the countryside badgers were regarded benignly and it was held that they did little or no damage to farmers.

There are many places in Irelandwhose names incorporate the word *broc*, the Irish word for badger. Such names include *Droumbrick*, The Badger's Ridge, *Beenabroc*, Badgers' Peak and *Dereenbrick*, The Badger's Wood. There is a lovely poem about the badger, written by John Clare.

The badger, according to tradition, had no back bone. When out of season there was a strong well-defined odour from them, an odour which had almost always disappeared by the time of the badger moon.

The flesh of the pig badger was believed to be good wholesome food. It was akin to the flesh of the pig and was very fat. The flesh of the dog badger was not eaten at all. The skin might be nailed to a door and dried, after which it might serve as a very efficient foot mat, though it took quite some considerable time to dry because of all the fat. The hair or bristles grew deep into the skin.

The meat of the badger was particularly flavoursome when boiled with cabbage, and was thought to contain a cure when cooked in this way. If after her confinement a mother did not regain her usual strength, she was restored to health and vigour by having some badger flesh boiled with cabbage. Even if she found the flesh too strong the cabbage alone restored her.

Badgers, like hares, were hunted with dogs. It was thought that if a badger took hold of a dog's leg he would not release his grip until he heard the bone in the leg snap beneath his teeth. Badgers were sold to fur shops and fetched about four shillings each around 1940. The following story illustrates the protectiveness of the badger towards its young:

In Shroneboy in the parish of Glenflesk lived a man named Fionán O'Donoghue. His farm included a mountain and he kept cattle and it was the duty of his son Patsy Fionáin to go to the hill each day and count the animals. Patsy was this time about eight or nine years old. One day he found two young badgers which he thought were pups and he brought them home. They were under a flat flag when he found them. When his father saw them he became alarmed and, accompanied by other men and dogs and armed with pikes, the young badgers were returned to the place where Patsy had found them. Seemingly if they were not returned, the young fellow could not go to count the animals for ages as the old badger would find the smell of the young ones from him and would attack him.

A woman who lived near our house when I was a child would never wander forth after dusk because she was afraid of the badgers and the 'pookies' though she never said which she feared most. There was, however, a story told of St Ciarán and the badger, showing the badger in a favourable light: St Ciarán lived in the woods and there, with the help of his animal friends, he established a monastery. One day the fox took one of the saint's sandals in his mouth and carried it off; the faithful badger raced after him, grabbed the culprit by the ear and obliged him to return the shoe to the saint.

* * *

The Hedgehog: The hedgehog with its spiny coat scarcely needs to be described. It hibernates in winter and during hibernation its temperature drops. It snuffles a great deal, however, when active and foraging for food. It was said to steal milk from cows in some parts of the country. Its most distinctive behaviour pattern is, of course, to roll itself into a ball for protection, when its sharp spines must surely seem intimidating even to the most fierce of predators.

Travellers were believed to be very fond of the flesh of the hedgehog. There was a fairly widespread belief that they rolled it up in a ball of clay and cooked it in that fashion. When the animal was cooked, the clay would crack, the spines and skin coming away with the clay. The flesh was then ready to be eaten.

* * *

The Shrew: The pigmy shrew is the smallest of all Irish mammals. One of its most discernible characteristics is its long snout which is both slender and flexible. Though much smaller, it is often confused with a mouse. In many parts of Ireland the shrew was held to be a relative of the weasel, which it is not. In olden times there was at least one curious superstition regarding this diminutive animal. A cow that had been walked upon or run upon by a shrew would develop terrible swellings and would die if immediate action were not taken to remedy the situation. Such a cow was said to be 'shrew-struck'. It was thought that the only way to save the cow's life was to burn the body of a shrew and apply the ashes to the swellings.

* * *

The Otter: The otter is related to both the stoat and the badger. It has webbed feet on its elongated body and its tail is long and flat. The otter eats a great variety of fish but in Irish tradition his speciality was the salmon. It was widely believed that when he grabbed a salmon, he turned it down with the flood, and the flooding waters choked the fish. It was easy for the otter to bring the salmon on land then. There is an account in *The Field* of 1881 which describes an otter attempting to catch two salmon at once:

> The first he seized hold of but after a severe struggle lasting several minutes it got away; he went in pursuit of the fish again and met a second salmon which after some hard work in a rapid stream he succeeded in mastering and carried to the

weirs where he left it on a wall. He then immediately returned to the spot where he had lost the first, and it was not this time able to make any fight owing to its previous injuries so that the otter carried him off where he had the other.

According to tradition, Lord Belmore of Florencecourt kept an otter as a pet and trained it to catch fish for him. The otter makes a fine repast on the salmon and other fish that have the misfortune to come its way, but it was commonly believed that the otter ate only the head of the salmon and shamefully abandoned the rest on some river bank or shore.

The otter is now a protected species but for many years it was hunted, perhaps because of its depredations of fishing stocks, though these depredations were at times grossly exaggerated. Its skin was also highly valued, and accounts of otter hunts were a regular feature of local newspapers throughout the nineteenth century and well into the twentieth century

An interesting tale of an otter hunter goes as follows:

Once there was a man who spent a great deal of his time hunting and killing otters. On one occasion he caught an otter and when he was removing it from the trap, the otter snapped at his hand and inflicted a deep wound. The man tried one remedy after another but none of them worked and there was no improvement in the condition of his hand. Then someone told him that he should kill another otter and eat the flesh and that would effect a cure. He did this and it is said that his hand was cured.

According to the old saying, the otter was one of three things that never rested – the others being a steep waterfall and a demon from hell.

* * *

The Fox: The fox, with his rich red fur and long bushy tail, is truly a most handsome animal. He figures prominently in Irish folklore. We have already described his adventures with the scaldcrow and the eagle, and in both of these stories he was cast in his familiar role – that of a wily and cunning fellow who always outwits his adversaries in the end. Strangely, however, he was duped by the cock when the cock escaped from the jaws of death in the third of our fox stories already outlined. A version of this tale was published in *Bealoideas* in December 1933.

'As cunning as a fox' is still a popular proverb. Another advised caution: 'The fox never found a better messenger than himself' but 'the fox that leaves the covert while the hounds are in the glen seals his own fate'.

Arthur Stringer wrote about the fox:

> A fox is certainly a very subtle creature and is very ravenous and will kill sheep, lambs, fawns, turkeys, geese, hens ducks, wild or tame, pheasants, partridge, woodcock, hares and rabbits, all of which he takes by policy in creeping under the wind so nigh them before they can fly or run away that he leaps upon them.

Stringer added that he knew of a case in which a fox had killed nineteen hens and two cocks in one night which he took out of a roost in a little hen house and then hid in ploughed ground under trees as well as in bushes within half a mile of the slaughter.

Foxes were held to be good parents; they fed their young even when times were lean and they went hungry themselves. It was believed that vixens regurgitated food for their young, a folk belief which is now accepted as fact by many experts. In some parts of Ireland it was thought that when a fox killed a bird such as a large goose, which was heavy and cumbersome, he grabbed the bird by the head and manoeuvred under her neck until he had managed to get her body to rest on his shoulders. There were many tales of the fox playing dead when caught red-handed (or should that be red-pawed?), as he raided the hen house. The luckless farmer invariably went off to share the good news with his family or went in search of a bag in which to deposit the dead fox but when he returned the fox had vanished.

There were tales too of foxes who, by their cunning, had found their way onto offshore islands:

> A fox living in Dursey sound saw the boats going into Dursey island and he thought in his own mind that perhaps if he could get in there that plenty of fowl would be had for the chasing. But that was the puzzle; how to get in. He was watching the boats every day leaving the shore and going in. So one day he lay down on the shore and let on to be dead. When the men came and saw the fox on the shore they were sure he was dead and they brought him onto the island for curiosity. On reaching the shore the men threw the fox overboard and *as go brách* [away] with the fox.

This story is well known by all the people of Cork and Kerry. A similar tale was told to explain how the first fox arrived in the Aran Islands when two boatmen from Rosamhíl brought what they thought was a dead fox to the port of Cill Ronáin. The fox made a great slaughter of ducks and geese, and dogs were sent after it. The dogs pursued the fox to a cliff named *An Troigh Mharbhtha.* The fox struggled down the cliff face, clinging to a briar which it held in its mouth, but the dogs in hot pursuit leapt to their deaths on the rocks below. More geese and ducks were killed by the fox; another pack pursued the wily fox over the cliff, but they too perished. The third night brings a further slaughter of farmyard birds, but by that time the fox's trick of taking the briar in its mouth had been discovered, and so the briar was cut before the final and fateful hunt. The fox led the third pack of hounds to the cliff, but the briar came away in its mouth and it fell to its death.

Here is another tale which illustrates the cunning of the fox:

> My uncle, Dan Downing Lohart, who is still alive and who lives in our house was a great sportsman in his day. Once upon a time he noticed a fox taking stones in his paw and settling them there well and then throwing up the stones at the fowl which perched on the branches of an oak tree which was about 70 feet or so from the ground. He did his best in this way to force down the fowl and if he failed it was not his fault.

There were several traditions with minute variations which described how the fox entered a dwelling house and how he effected his escape, but in almost all of them Reynard had recourse to the threat of fire:

> Foxes are scarce but they sometimes come and steal the poultry. This is a story about one of their clever tricks. A man lived in Doire na mBreac about 70 years ago called Pat Thade. One day it happened that Pat went out to the well for a pail of spring water and when he came back to the house there was a fox before him and he tried to shut the door to catch the fox. A sheaf of oats lay on the kitchen floor and also a cradle with a baby in it. The fox ran towards the fire dragging the sheaf with him; he lit it and the man thought he was going to burn the child to death. So he ran to save the child and off ran the fox out the door saving his life by a clever trick.

In another version the fox came through a hole in the door which had been reserved for use by the household dogs which were now not at home. The owner of the house rushed towards the door and began to whistle for his dogs, whereupon the fox promptly took a burning log from the hearth and directed his steps towards the bed beside the fire. His opponent feared that he would set the house ablaze, so he abandoned his place at the door and the fox escaped.

In another tale, a king proclaimed his tolerance far and wide and promised his kingdom to anyone who would tempt him to say 'You lie'. Indeed, the king was a tolerant fellow for he was obliged to listen to a litany of exaggerated stories and never once did he feel the slightest inclination to say 'You lie'. Then a youth came before him and for a long time it seemed as if he would enjoy as little success as his predecessors. At length, the youth came to the part of his story which told how he had seen a red fox scampering away through the grasses. The youth had given hot pursuit and, after a long chase, he had grabbed the handsome fox by his long bushy tail. The poor fox had been very frightened, gasping and coughing and spluttering pitifully until at last he brought up a heap of books.

'Indeed?' said the king with sudden interest.

'Well I took up one of the books and I opened it and what do you think I read there?'

'What?' asked the king.

'That your father was in service to my father.'

'You lie,' said the king, and the youth smiled at his own success for none could keep the kingdom or the princess from him now.

The tongue of the fox was believed to contain a cure for many ailments. If, for instance you had an obstinate thorn in your foot, a thorn that could not be removed, a suitable remedy would be to rub the affected area with the tongue of a fox, and this procedure would bring forth the thorn. Foxes, it was believed had originally been dogs brought by the Vikings to Ireland.

Foxes are good swimmers but here is a very colourful folktale which purported to explain how the fox rid himself of fleas:

> The way a fox takes the fleas out of himself is: he gets a mouthful of wool on a hedge where there are sheep and he goes to the bank of a river and 'sets' back slowly into the water. The fleas creep up along his back. He keeps setting back along the water until all the fleas are up on his head. He then puts his head under the water and leaves the wool cocking up. All the fleas go into the wool and it floats away carrying all the fleas with it!

This belief was very popular in many areas, though in some parts it was said that the fox had to perform the operation with the wool three times before he had finally said goodbye to all his fleas.

The fox hunt was once a favourite pastime of the Irish landed gentry, though Oscar Wilde wittily described fox hunting as 'the unspeakable in pursuit of the uneatable'. Phantom fox hunts were not unknown in Ireland, particularly in the environs of long-deserted stately homes, when ghostly riders with their horses and hounds pursued their elusive quarry – all like fleeting shadows driven by the wind as they passed before the gaze of some bewildered observer.

The foxes at Gormanstown were particularly celebrated, and this was scarcely surprising since the crest of the Viscounts of Gormanstown featured a motif depicting a running fox. Gormanstown Castle is located in County Meath and it was said that when the master of the house died, the foxes in the immediate environs all left their dens and gathered around the castle. Apparently the foxes came in pairs and then took their places in an orderly way beneath the bedroom window where they howled and cried all night long. One remarkable feature of their behaviour, it was said, was that they completely ignored all poultry and game birds in the vicinity while they in turn were treated with extraordinary indifference by the castle dogs. But why did the foxes come to the funerals of the Viscounts of Gormanstown? It was believed that hundreds of years before, one of the incumbents of the castle came upon a vixen stoutly defending her litter against the approach of the pack, whereupon the benign gentleman immediately called off his hounds. The foxes were grateful for this kindness and duly lamented the passing of the kind old Viscount when he passed away some years later. Successive generations of foxes faithfully upheld this honourable tradition.

Foxes were very clever in their dealings with traps. They generally sprang traps by dropping stones or sticks onto them. They also figured prominently in the folk customs of fisherfolk, right along the western seaboard, especially in counties Galway and Mayo. O'Donovan described one belief thus:

> There is a most extraordinary superstition still deep rooted in the minds of all the fishermen in Galway, Aran and Connemara; they cannot bear to hear the name of a fox, hare or rabbit

pronounced and should they chance to see any of these animals living or dead or hear the name of either expressed before setting out to fish in the morning they would not venture out that day.

Thus, if a fisherman from the Claddagh on his way to the strand caught sight of a fox, he would return home without putting out to sea. This was the formula used by malevolent persons to ensure that the fishermen would have no luck:

> Sionnach ar do dhubhá; giorria ar do bhaoite;
> 's ná mharbha tú aon bhreac
> as seo go Lá Fhéile Bhríde.
> (A fox on your fishing hook, a hare on your bait
> May you kill no trout from this till St Brigid's day.)

Amongst the games played at Irish wakes was one called Fox Harra. Young men and young women formed a circle as they sat on some straw which was strewn on the floor. Then someone came and scattered more straw over their legs. One of those in the circle took possession of a shoe which was then passed from one player to another as furtively as possible beneath the straw, each one tossing the straw to confuse the player who stood in the centre, sometimes called the leader – and whose aim it was to determine which player had the shoe in his grasp at any given moment in time. When the leader eventually discovered the correct location of the shoe, the one who had been discovered holding the shoe might be required to undergo some humiliation or might simply be required to take the place of the leader in the centre of the circle.

There was also a game called Fox and Hounds in which a group of players stood in a line, each one behind the other, their legs wide apart. At one end of the line stood 'the fox' and at the other end 'the hound'. The hound soon gave chase but was only allowed to move in the same direction as his quarry, thus preventing him from wheeling suddenly and grabbing the unsuspecting fox. The chase might move around the line of standing players or between their legs. The hound was allowed three chases to catch the fox; if he failed to do so within that span of time, the fox might go free if he wished and another fox might take his place. Only when he had captured one fox or another might the hound depart from the game.

* * *

The Mouse: It was believed that when a dormouse walked over a cow the animal became crippled. The owner of the cow should then take off his shirt and make nine knots with it, striking the animal nine times, repeating each time: 'In the name of the Father and of the Son and of the Holy Spirit'. If a dead mouse was boiled in milk and the resulting concoction imbibed, this would prove to be a very effective cure for maladies including whooping cough and measles.

The mouse was one of the principal players in Patrick Kennedy's well-loved tale of The Grateful Beasts:

There was once a young man and it happened that he had a guinea in his pocket and was going to some fair or pattern or another and while he was on the way he saw some little boys scourging a poor mouse they had caught. 'Here boys,' says he, 'don't be so cruel. Here's sixpence for you to buy gingerbread and let him go.' They only wanted the wind of the word and off jumped the mouse. He didn't go much further when he overtook another crowd of young lads and they tormenting the life out of a poor weasel. Well he bought him off for a shilling and went on. The third creature he rescued from a gathering of grown-up young scoundrels was a donkey and he had to give a whole half crown to have him spared. 'Now,' says poor Neddy, 'you may as well take me with you. I'll be of some use carrying you when you're tired.' 'With all my heart,' says Jack. The day was very hot and the boy sat under the tree to enjoy the shade. As soon as he did he fell asleep without intending it but he was soon awakened by a wicked looking *bodach* and his two servants. 'How dare you let your ass trespass on my land,' says he to Jack, 'and do such mischief.'

'I had no notion he'd do anything of the kind. I dropped asleep by accident.'

'Oh be this and be that, I'll accidence you. Bring out that chest,' says he to one of the servants, and while you'd be saying thrapsticks they had the poor boy lying on the broad of his back in it and a strong hempen rope tied round it, and himself an itself flung into the river.

Well they went away about their business and poor Neddy stayed roaring and bawling on the bank, till who should come up but the weasel and the mouse and they axed him what ailed him. 'An' isn't that kind lad that rescued me from them scoggins that were tormenting me just now fastened up in a chest and driven' down that terrible river?'

'Oh,' says the weasel, 'he must be the same lad that rescued the mouse and myself. Had he a brown patch on the elbow of his coat?'

'The very same.'

'Come then,' says the weasel, 'and let us overtake him and get him out.'

'By all means,' says the others. So the weasel got on the ass' back and the mouse in his ear and away with them.

They hadn't the trouble of going far when they seen the chest which was lodged amongst the rushes at the edge of a little island. Over they went and the weasel and the mouse gnawed the rope until they had the lid off and their master went out on the bank. Well they were all very glad and were conversing together when what should the weasel spy but a beautiful egg with the loveliest colours on the shell lying down in the shallow water? It wasn't long till he had it up and Jack was turning it round and round and admiring it. 'Oh musha, my good friends', says he. 'I wish it was in my power to show my gratitude to you and that we had a fine castle and estate where we could live with full and plenty.'

The words were hardly out of his mouth when the beasts and himself found themselves standing on the steps of a castle and the grandest lawn before them that ever was seen. There was no one inside or outside to dispute possession with them and there they lived as happy as kings. They found plenty of money inside in a cupboard and the house had the finest furniture in every room and it was an easy matter to hire servants and labourers.

Jack was standing at his gate one day as three merchants were passing with their goods packed on the backs of horses and mules. 'Death alive,' says they. 'What's this for? There was neither castle nor lawn nor tree here the last time we went by.'

'True for you,' says Jack. 'But you won't be the worse for it. Take your beasts into the bawn behind the house and give them a good feed and if you're not in a hurry stay and take a bit of dinner with myself.' They wished for no better and after dinner the innocent slob of a Jack let himself be overtaken, and showed them his painted egg and told them everything that happened to him. As sure as the hearth money, one of them put a powder in Jack's next tumbler and when he woke it was in the island he found himself with his patched coat on him and his three friends sitting on their haunches near him and looking very down in the mouth.

'Oh, master,' says the weasel. 'You'll never be wise enough for the tricky people in the world. Where did them thieves say they lived and what's the name they had on them?' Jack scratched his head and after a while remembered the town. 'Come, Neddy,' says the weasel. 'Let us be jogging.' So he got on his back and the mouse in his ear and the ass swam the river and nothing is said of their travels till they came to the house of the head rogue. The mouse went in and the ass and the weasel sheltered themselves in a copse outside. He soon came back to them.

'Well what news?'

'Dull enough news. He has the egg in a low press in his bedroom and a pair of cats with fiery eyes watching it night and day and they chained to the press and the room door double locked,' says the mouse.

'Let us go back,' says the ass. 'We can do nothing.'

'Wait!' says the weasel.

When sleep time came, says the weasel to the mouse: 'Go in at the keyhole and get behind the rogue's head and stay two or three hours sucking his hair.'

'Where's the good in that?' says the mouse.

'Wait and you'll know,' says the weasel.

Next morning the merchant was quite mad to find the way his hair was in. 'But I'll disappoint you tonight, you thief of a mouse,' says he, so he unchained the cats next night and bid them sit by his bed to watch.

Just as he was dropping asleep, the weasel and the mouse were outside the door and gnawing away till they had a hole scooped out at the bottom. In went the mouse and it wasn't long till he had the egg outside. They were soon on the road again; the mouse in the ass' ear, the weasel on his back and the egg in the weasel's mouth. When they came to the river and were swimming across, the ass began to bray: 'Is there the likes of me in the world? I'm carrying the mouse and the weasel and the great enchanted egg that can do anything. Why don't ye praise me?' He paused. 'I'll shake ye off ye ungrateful pack if ye don't,' says the ass again, and the misfortunate weasel, forgetting himself, shouted out, 'No don't', and down went the precious egg into the deepest pool of the river.

'Now you've done it,' says the weasel, and you may be sure the donkey looked very down cast.

'Oh what are we to do now at all at all?' says he.

'Never despair,' says the weasel. He looked down into the deep water and cried: 'Hear all you frogs and fishes. There is a great army coming to take ye away and eat ye right now; look sharp.'

'Oh and what can we do?' says they coming up to the surface.

'Gather up all the stones and hand them to us and we'll make a big wall on the bank to defend ye.'

They went to work like little divils in a mud wall and were hard and fast reaching up the pebbles they found in the bottom. At last a big frog came up with the egg in his mouth and when the weasel had hold of it he got up on a tree and cried out: 'That will do. The army is frightened and running away.' So the poor things were greatly relieved.

You may be sure that Jack was very rejoiced to see his friends and the egg again. They were soon back in the castle and lawn and when Jack began to feel lonesome he did not find it hard to make out a fine young wife for himself, and his three friends were as happy as the day was long.

It was said that St Canice of Kilkenny banished mice and rats from his island hermitage.

The mouse figured in old sayings such as 'As timid as a mouse', and 'What should a cat do but hunt mice?' and 'Two cats with the one mouse will never agree.'

A mouse and a frog fell into a gallon of sour milk and they were sure they would drown. At first the mouse thought he would drink some of the milk but it was very sour and, besides, if he drank it all he would burst. The frog kept leaping up and down all the time struggling to reach the top of the gallon, though any fool could see it was hopeless for wasn't the gallon a big tall thing? The mouse leapt for a while but then gave up, said his prayers and drowned. The frog seemed a right fool for says he to himself, 'Never say never say die', and he kept on jumping till the bitter end till he had all the cream turned to butter, and then he used the butter as a springboard and leapt to safety. The moral of this story: 'God loves a trier.'

Rats: The brown rat has long been regarded with loathing by the people of the countryside. When I was a child my mother had a rhyme which depicted the rat as being somewhat bewildered at human hostility towards him:

> A frog and a rat were out walking one day
> 'Kind sir,' says the rat, 'please tell me I pray
> Why all the people are civil to you,
> But look upon me as if death were my due?'
> Said Froggie, 'My friend, the reason is clear,
> Water is cheap but the grain is dear,
> If you only took water and mud and such stuff
> The people to you would be civil enough.'

There was a time when the cat and the rat behaved with great civility towards one another and one day they went to the fair. They went into a public house and came upon a barrel of whiskey in a back room. The rat made a hole in the barrel and pretended to drink some of the whiskey, inviting his companion to do likewise, but the cat was reluctant to do so. The latter was afraid that he might get drunk and might fall off the chair into the fire when he got home. The rat urged him at least to have a little drop for the road – a little drop would give them both courage. If the cat did fall into the fire, his bosom pal, the rat, would pull him out again, on condition that the cat gave an undertaking that he would never interfere with the rat or his kind again. The cat went home and fell asleep in the chair and he soon fell into the fire. The rat let him have a good roasting before he took him out so that the cat was very much the worse for wear, not only from the flames but also from his spree in the town. The rats young and old had great fun round the house. They broke cups and saucers by the new time, and the people of the house were very upset. The woman of the house could see that the cat had something of a hangover so she doused him with a couple of buckets of water, and the hapless feline came to his senses again. The chase began, and from that time onwards there was never any peace between the rat and the cat. The story of the rat charmer, a variation on the Pied Piper, was also popular in Ireland. The Rat Charmer could by means of enchantment lead away a plague of unwanted rats!

Whenever anyone abandoned a project which seemed doomed to failure they were said to be like rats fleeing a sinking ship. Rats on ships were known as 'cowld irons'. Many of the ships which transported Irish 'convicts' to Australia in the late eighteenth century were infested with rats, as indeed were many merchant and cargo ships of the period. There are a number of variations of the tale which describes how, when his ship was plagued with rats, the frustrated captain placed a notice in a newspaper offering a reward to anyone who would rid him of them. The pied piper in this case was a young man but he did not whistle a tune. Rather he deposited a large razor blade in an upright position on the deck and began to read from a holy book, whereupon the rats came forth one by one and nonchalantly proceeded to cut their own throats on the sharpened edge of the blade.

The rat was one of the players in the whimsical tale of 'The Wonderful Cake' written by Patrick Kennedy:

> A mouse, a rat and a little red hen once lived together in the same cottage and one day the little red hen said, 'Let us bake a cake and have a feast.'
>
> 'Let us,' says the mouse, and 'Let us,' says the rat.
>
> 'Who shall go and get the wheat ground?' says the hen.
>
> 'I won't,' says the mouse, and 'I won't,' says the rat.
>
> 'I will myself,' says the little red hen. 'Who'll make the cake?'

'I won't,' says the mouse, and 'I won't,' says the rat.

'I will myself,' says the little red hen.

Well, while the hen was stretching her hand out for it 'hey presto', out rolled the cake from the cottage and after it ran the mouse, the rat and the little red hen. When it was running away it went by a barn full of threshers and they asked where it was running. 'Oh,' says it, 'I'm running away from the mouse, the rat and the little red hen and you too if I can.' Well they all ran after it along with the rest till it came to a well full of washers and they asked the same question and it returned the same answer and after it they went. At last it came to a ford where it met with a fox who asked where it was running. 'Oh, I'm running away from the mouse, the rat and the little red hen, and from a barn full of threshers, a ditch full of ditchers, a well full of washers and from you too if I can.'

'But you can't cross the ford,' says the fox.

'And can't you carry me over?' says the cake.

'What'll you give me?' says the fox.

'A kiss at Christmas and an egg at Easter,' says the cake.

'Very well,' says the fox. 'Up with you.' So he sat on his haunches with his nose in the air and the cake got up by his tail till it sat on his crupper.

'Now over with you,' says the cake.

'You're not high enough,' says the fox. Then it scrambled up on his shoulders. 'Up higher still,' says he, 'You wouldn't be safe there.'

'Am I right now?' says the cake.

'Nearly, but not quite. You'll be safer on the ridge pole of my nose.'

'Well,' says the cake, 'I think I can go no further.'

'Oh yes you can,' says the fox and he shot it up in the air, caught it with his mouth and sent it down the little red lane and that was the end of the wonderful cake.

The notion of plagues and infestations of loathsome creatures visited on wrongdoers occurs more than once in the Bible. The same theme also found a place in Irish folklore:

This woman who refused to have stations in her house was visited by 7 rats of different colours. They always disappeared when the sacrifice of the Mass was being offered up in a church nearby. Some time afterwards there came a priest to the parish who offered to banish the rats but as penance the woman was required to draw huge stones down from a mountain and place them about her house. In normal circumstances it would have taken three strong men to lift one of these rocks but the luckless woman lifted them with great difficulty. She sometimes sat on top of the rocks to rest and was seen rocking herself to and fro in her distress as her neighbours made their way to Mass.

Apart from music and prayers the most popular way of getting rid of rats was to write them a letter and to deposit the letter in a place where they were sure to see it. The letter should state that the rats had overstayed their welcome but that they would find suitable lodgings in an alternative place. This latter place had to be named and had to be supplied with adequate provisions. A grain store would be the ideal choice in such circumstances.

There were a number of tales which told how the first rats and cats came into being:

Once upon a time there was a man who was able to work some kind of charm. One day his wife and himself were going begging and they went into a miller's house looking for a grain of flour. They got the flour and after they went out, the house was full of flour. Martin, which was the miller's name, ran after them with a bucket of flour and when he was just crossing the fence he tore all his chest with a briar. The old man picked a little buttercup and rubbed it to Martin's chest and it got better. He told him to keep his hat under the table and when he got up in the morning something good would be there. When Martin got up in the morning a sow with a fine litter of bonhams was there. Some time later Martin met the old man again and told him about the great thing that had just happened. The old man again told him to put his hat under the table and when he awoke in the morning he was glad to find a lovely grey sheepdog with seven pups under the table. But now, Kate, the servant girl, grew jealous. When she was going to bed that night she put her cap under the table and to her surprise when she got up in the morning a rat with about fourteen ugly young rats was under the table. She was preparing to go to Mass and she threw a glove at them and the rat changed into a cat and killed all the young ones.

* * *

Deer: We have already recounted the tale of the robins advice in which three sons set out to seek their fortune and encountered a hag in the form of a hare who lured them to her cabin in the woods. In other versions of the same tale, the hag took the form of a deer.

Enchanted does, always white, were occasionally seen. The deer figured in sayings such as 'Often the hound that was mocked killed the deer.' The native red deer abounds in the mountains about Killarney and the stag hunt was one of the principal amusements of the area in the Victorian period. The stag hunt figured prominently in the legend of O'Sullivan's

Cascade. It was customary for Victorian guide books to point out that the waters of the cascade rushed downwards from a lake in the hollow of the hill, called O'Sullivan's Punchbowl. The O'Sullivans, the tourist was assured, were 'grate chieftains in the ould times and had royal blood in their veins'. They owned a great stretch of land about the lakes, 'but their hearts were too big for their manes and they were obligated to sell this part of the mountain to Mr Herbert of Muckross.' The story went on:

> A long time before there was a waterfall here at all, one of the rale ould O'Sullivans was out all day hunting the red deer. Well just as he was getting weary what should O'Sullivan see but the most beautiful stag that ever was seen before or since in the world. For he was as big as a colt and he had horns upon him like a weaver's beam and a collar of rale red gold round his neck. Away went the stag and away went the dogs after him in full cry. And O'Sullivan after the dogs for he was determined to have the beautiful stag. The stag never stopped nor stayed till he came to the place where the Punchbowl is now. When O'Sullivan came to the same place he was fairly ready to drop. But the stag was nowhere to be seen high nor low. Seeing there was no use in staying there he whistled his dogs and was just going to go home when who should he meet but Finn Mac Cumhal. 'What do you want with me?' says O'Sullivan puttin' on as bould a face as he could.
>
> 'I want to know what business you had hunting my stag,' says Finn. 'If it was anywan else but yourself I'd play the red vengeance with him. But as you're wan of the right sort and my stag has led you a pretty dance I'll give you a drop of good drink.' Then Finn Mac Cumhal stamped his foot and all of a sudden, just in the hollow which his feet made, there came up a little lake which tumbled down the mountainside and made the waterfall. When O'Sullivan went to take a drink of it, what should it be but the rale whiskey punch and it stayed running with whiskey until the Sassenachs came into the country and all at wance it turned into water again.

* * *

Rabbits: There were not nearly as many superstitions about the rabbit as there were about the hare. There was an old saying which linked the two together: 'The rabbit gets fat on what the hare misses.' However, a lone rabbit was a sign of bad luck especially for the fishermen.

Snaring rabbits was a favourite occupation of young boys in some country places. Four wires about eighteen inches long were first twisted together. A loop was made in one end, the other end being pulled through and fastened to a rope which was afterwards secured to a peg driven into the ground. The wire portion was raised slightly off the ground by a slender stick. The loop was adjusted to the size of the rabbit's head and placed in a likely place. When the hapless rabbit stepped into the loop it tightened about his neck and killed him.

It was held in some parts that snow-white rabbits were scattered amongst their more orthodox fellows. These white rabbits were very particular about their fur and were very loathe to sully it. One method of capturing these rarities was to place some mud and grime outside their burrows. Then none of the animals would try to escape as they would be afraid they might dirty their fur.

There was a tale of how a poor boy used rabbits to outwit a landlord.

> The boy and his mother had been evicted from their cottage and they would only be allowed to return if the boy did good deeds. One of the challenges issued by the landlord to the boy was that he should take the horse from under the plough without the knowledge of the ploughman. The boy captured some rabbits and took them to the field whereupon the plough-man ran after them and the boy unharnessed the horse. Thereafter the boy and his mother were allowed to return to their cottage.

A Kilkenny variation of this folktale appeared in *Bealoideas* in 1932.

Another story heard in the country was that of Muddy Paws, the rabbit who always got mud in his paws despite repeated warnings from his mother. One day a wily fox followed the muddy footprints to the door of the burrow and the entire family would surely have been devoured by the predator were it not for the diversion created by the heroic father. Maybe there was a moral there somewhere for little boys with messy hands.

* * *

Hares: This was the riddle about the hare: 'A hopper of ditches, a cutter of corn, a brown little cow without any horns.' Most of us have heard the saying, 'As swift as a hare', but there were others too such as 'Tis hard to drive the hare from a bush she's not in.'

The most popular tradition relating to the hare was that it

milked cows especially on May mornings. These cow-milking hares were really hags and witches who had taken that form through some enchantment. There were tales of farmers who were mystified that their prize cows suddenly showed a marked and sustained decrease in the level of their milk production. Eventually, the farmer maintained a nocturnal vigil when he observed the hare approaching to milk the cow, and the riddle was finally solved. Sometimes the farmer fired a shot at the hare, and sometimes it turned into a hag before his eyes, but there were always traces of blood on the ground.

The Irish hare is an endemic subspecies of the arctic hare and is quite different from the mountain hare. The Irish species is smaller than the brown, its ears are much shorter and its tail is dazzlingly white. Sir William Wilde observed with regard to the widespread superstitition concerning the hag hare: 'On May day likewise if they find a hare among their herd, they endeavour to kill her out of a notion that it is some old witch that has a design upon their butter.' In some few areas it was the hedgehog and not the hare that milked the cows. Paradoxically, it was unlucky to kill a hare before sunrise. If one met a hare when setting out on a journey one should turn back as the hare presaged some untoward incident.

There were many tales of enchanted gatherings of hares. Here is an interestng story from County Limerick.

Some years ago there lived an old woman near the village of Athea. She lived in a small thatched house with her son, a tailor. She used to turn herself into a magic hare by means of a cow's horn which she kept in the thatch. Her son was working with a tailor in Rusoa. On one occasion the two tailors came to the old woman's house. They were sleeping in a little room over the kitchen and they could see all that was going on in the kitchen. About twelve o'clock the old woman went up on the table and took down the cow's horn and rubbed it to her forehead and immediately she turned into a hare. She went away out and did not return till three o'clock. The (visiting) tailor did not sleep till she came back. When she came back she went up on the table and took down the cow's horn again and immediately she changed into an old woman. The visitor was thinking what he should do. So the next night he pretended to be in bed but again he watched the old woman's movements. She did the same thing as the night before and when she was gone, the tailor came down and did the same and turned himself into a hare, and out after the old woman. He followed her until he got up to her and they were talking until they came to a pier of a gate and she sat up on it and he sat up on the other one. Then she began to whistle and called all the other hares to her. Then all the hares gathered round her and one of them, the leader, said: 'I cannot tell you anything tonight because there is one here who does not belong to my flock, and they all disappeared and the old woman came off and ran off for the house and the tailor after her. She went in and got the horn and changed herself into an old woman. After a while the tailor came in and changed himself back again, but he had been so frightened by what had happened that he never followed the old woman again.

Those who hunted hares often had strange experiences. Here is just one example:

Long ago there lived a man in this neighbourhood by the name of O'Sullivan. This man was very fond of hunting and used to spend all his time out on the mountains with his hounds. One day when he was out a beautiful hare rose before him. The dogs immediately gave chase and O'Sullivan who was very fleet of foot followed close behind. The chase lasted for several hours and in the evening the hare disappeared. O'Sullivan turned to come home but at that moment he heard someone call to him. When he turned round he saw a beautiful lady dressed in white standing on a rock. The lady said to him: 'Why do you follow my hare?' and O'Sullivan said he thought that the hare was not owned by anyone. These words seemed to please the lady and, taking a mug of milk, she gave it to him and said: 'Take a drink for I know you are thirsty.' When O'Sullivan put the mug to his lips he was changed into a bird and he flew back to his own house. When the woman of the house saw the bird she caught it and killed it. The man then took his own form again and he told her the whole story.

In another story two huntsmen and their dogs walked through a field adjacent to a graveyard. One of the dogs ran into the graveyard, killed a hare and returned to his owner with the hare in his mouth. The man who owned the dog took the hare and brought it home with him. After a little while he got a severe pain in his hand, and at length he was treated by some of the finest surgeons in Dublin. He was, however, forced to return home, his hand incurable, with the result that with time his withered hand actually rotted off his body. He died soon afterwards and the storyteller concluded that it 'was the general view in the locality that there was something unhealthy in that hare'.

White hares like white rabbits were rarities indeed but they too figured in the tales:

There was a man one time in the parish of Kilmoyley who was a mystery man. He never spoke to anybody. He was a dark silent individual. He never spent a night in bed. It was thought he used to spend the night killing hares with a heavy stick which was, as the story went, always covered with blood. However, he died and the strangest thing about him was, on the day of his funeral a white hare came across the fields and sat down on the ditch in front of the cabin where he was laid out and being coffined, and nothing daunted by all the people around him. After looking right into the corpse for some time, he jogged slowly across the field again. However, there was a man looking on who had a great taste for game. He went to his home, took his greyhound with him, pursued the hare and finally killed it, with the result that he went insane and had to be taken to an asylum immediately.

If a pregnant mother encountered a hare, her child might be born with a harelip. Even a hare killed by a huntsman could cause this condition in the baby if the hare's tail had not been removed before being brought into the presence of the expectant mother.

* * *

The Goat: The bladder of a goat featured in a colourful if unorthodox cure for baldness. It was filled with human urine and suspended in the chimney above the fire, only being removed when quite dry. It was then ground down and rubbed vigorously into the scalp with slices of raw onion. The treatment was held to be quite effective.

The milk of the goat was held to be resistant against tuberculosis at a time when TB was rampant in the country, and so its consumption was highly recommended. It was also recommended for children suffering from skin diseases such as eczema.

The goat becomes king during Puck Fair which is held each year in August in the County Kerry town of Killorglin. The fair lasts for three days – the gathering day when the goat is crowned and enthroned on high on a lofty stand from which his majesty must surely observe the milling crowds beneath him with some bemusement; the fair day which brings the main business of the fair, the buying and selling of horses, and the scattering day when King Puck is dethroned and returned to his home in the mountains.

There was a great deal of local lore surrounding the reasons for the establishment of the fair. One theory was that the fair was called Puck Fair simply because the only animal offered for sale at the first fair in Killorglin was an old goat. Another theory held that the fair was a relic of some ancient pagan ritual associated with the festival of *Lughnasa*, one of the four great festivals of Celtic Ireland. Yet another theory insisted that Oliver Cromwell had a central role in the establishment of the fair. This told how Cromwell's soldiers frightened a herd of goats on Carran Tuathal and the herd dashed for Killorglin. The people of Killorglin thus heard of the approach of the soldiers and defended their town successfully against them. Thereafter they saw fit to enthrone a goat each August in memory of that victory. Goats were said to be able to digest almost anything and there were colourful stories about their strange eating habits. The town on the Laune was not the only town, however, to pay homage to the goat.

A goat was also enthroned at the fair in Mullinavat, Co Kilkenny at one time. According to one old saying, there was no point in going to the goat's shed if one was looking for wool, while another suggested that if one put silk on a goat he was still a goat. In some parts it was held that the first goat had been introduced into Ireland by the devil.

One popular custom was to put a goat in the field with the cows when they were put out to grass. It was said that this precaution would prevent the cows from slinking. The latter term was used when a cow calved before her time. When this happened the small farmer might suffer a substantial loss as the calf was generally dead, and the cow apparently yielded very little milk for some considerable time thereafter.

There was a foolish boy there long ago. One day as he was travelling along the road he found some pieces of gold under a stone. He thought the glittering fragments were nothing more than chainies so he brought some home in his pocket to show his mother. She was overjoyed when she saw the gold and gave her son a bag, telling him to go back and fill the bag with the remaining 'chainies'. He did this and the poor woman, poor no longer, had soon deposited her bag of gold in a large trunk. The day afterwards the landlord's agent came to the cottage. The mother was out searching for a hen's nest and the foolish boy asked the stranger if he was looking for his bag of chainies. The agent did not understand but said he would like to see the chainies. The boy led him towards the chest and threw back the lid. Soon the greedy agent was feasting his gaze on the golden coins, but just at that moment the mother returned. She pushed the agent into the chest and bolted it tightly. The agent duly suffocated, and when he was quite dead the distraught mother buried him in a hole in the garden. Unknown to her, the fool observed her from a distance as she worked. However, the next day when the boy was down by the river the mother took the precaution of digging up the agent again and burying him elsewhere depositing the body of an old goat in the first grave. A sergeant came making enquiries about the disappearance of the agent and, rather predictably, the fool told him that his mother had buried him in a hole in the garden. The sergeant set to work and began to dig. It was some time before he came upon the body of the old goat. 'This is the man, the man with the horns,' the fool said. The sergeant laughed and went away.

* * *

Sheep: It was considered bad luck to meet a flock of sheep coming towards one early in the morning. Conversely, it was good luck to see a flock of sheep some distance behind one on the road in the evening. Sheep were held to thrive better on land that was hard and dry rather than on land that was soggy and damp. In mountainy districts in particular, sheep represented the main source of income, the flock being driven onto the higher slopes during the summer months and being brought down to the lowlands during the winter. Every flock owner had a number of marks which distinguished his sheep from those of his neighbours. A different mark or letter might be burned into the right or left horn with a reddened brand. A tiny notch might be cut from the right or left ear. There was also a shoulder mark which was applied by daubing tar or paint onto the wool. It was said that the men who tended the sheep on the mountains had eyes like hawks and so they quickly missed a sheep that strayed.

The sheep was valued not only for its mutton but also for its wool. The fat sheep were taken to the fair at the crossroads or in the village, and were generally sold to butchers. Sheep were generally shorn twice a year and the wool might be sold to woollen mills which manufactured woollen yarns. Sometimes the wool was not offered for sale but was spun and woven by the women of the house. The fleece was washed and put out to dry, the women teasing the wool with their fingers in order to facilitate the drying process. When dry, more vigorous teasing was effected by the use of carders, after which the wool was ready for spinning and weaving. The cloth was very durable and almost impervious to rain, as the natural oils in the wool had not been removed by chemical processes.

There was a tradition on the islands along the western seaboard that the knitting which was done after dark was best because the sheep were then asleep. There were plenty of crickets round the hearth too, but the islanders never interfered with them, for if one injured a cricket his fellows would wreak vengeance by devouring large holes in the fine woollen garments of the offender. If the first lamb of the season was a black lamb, then the people of the house would be wearing mourning clothes before the year had ended. In the same way, it was very lucky to meet a white lamb first thing in the morning especially one with the sun shining directly on its face.

It was said of a boastful fellow that there were two heads on all his sheep. Another old saying which encouraged an adventurous approach to life was: 'You might as well be hung for a sheep as a lamb', but one with an ominous ring to it proclaimed: 'You can never tell whose skin will hang first from the rafter – the old sheep or the lamb.' Yet another asserted: 'There was never a scabby sheep that didn't have a comrade.'

One of the most popular symbols for Christ was the Lamb. An old folktale offered a reason for this:

> When our Lord was born in that cold bleak stable in Bethlehem he had an enemy named Herod. One day Herod ordered his soldiers to search Bethlehem for the Christ Child and to put him to death. News of this reached Mary, the Virgin Mother. She threw a cloak round herself and the child and she hurried off with him. She travelled as fast as she could. At length then, troubled and weary, she had to sit down and rest and it was not long until she heard the soldiers approach. She could see no place in which she might hide but she placed her trust in God that he might come to her aid. She cradled the child in her apron. The soldiers came and asked her what she had in the apron. She opened the apron for them and what was inside but a handsome little lamb? The captain ordered his men to proceed. The Virgin kissed the lamb and gave thanks to God for the miracle he had wrought.

In another version of the story it was the adult Christ who was pursued by the soldiers. When the soldiers drew near he went into a field and took the form of a little lamb, whereupon the soldiers passed by without realising that their quarry was near at hand. This was why sheep and lambs were held to be especially blessed by God.

The method for curing mange in sheep, as well as in other animals, was to place three spoons of sulphur into a bottle of train oil. Then the bottle was given a vigorous shake and, when the affected area had been thoroughly washed with hot water, the mixture of sulphur and train oil was applied with a soft clean cloth. A less popular method involved a solution of lime water and turpentine. Yellow flowers such as those of the ragwort were fed to sheep with liver fluke but this seems to have been a fairly inneffectual remedy.

* * *

Horses: In the days before the tractor, a good horse was highly prized and well cared for. The majority of farmers kept at least two horses. During the winter months the horses might spend much of their time in the stable, while during the summer they grazed in the fields. A manger was filled with hay for each horse in the stable and the horses might be tied with a halter, though in many instances if there was only one horse, the animal was left loose around the stable. When a mare foaled the membraneous covering around the new arrival was generally dried and preserved and hung somewhere about the stable to bring luck to the horses.

The horse was shod at the forge once a month and there might be four or six forges in a parish. Amongst the implements used in the forge were the bellows for fanning the fire, and the anvil on which the red hot metal was hammered and shaped. The blacksmith also had an array of hammers, large and small, as well as a type of circular knife which was used for paring the hoofs of horses and colts. In addition, he had a rasp and a file, also for paring. The 'Punch' was used for making holes in hot iron, and the drill for making holes in cold iron. The pincers and tongs served to remove the iron from the fire. Horse shoe nails were stored in the box with the rasp, the knife and the hammers. Not only did the smith make ploughs and harrows, he also repaired them and a great many other farm implements. He was further required to fit bands on the wheels of carts.

Forge water was held to be an effective remedy for cattle suffering from the red murrain. At one time the blessed Virgin came to a forge seeking a pin with which she might fasten her shawl. The smith was only too happy to oblige the mother of God. He took the nearest piece of metal to hand, and it wasn't long before he had set to work. About a half an hour later he had a fine pin made. When he plunged the pin into the water to cool the metal, he noticed that the tiredness left his limbs and he felt utterly refreshed. From that time onwards, however weary a blacksmith might feel, the tiredness would aways leave his body when he placed his hands in the forge water.

A favourite motif in Irish folklore was that of the water steed who came out of sea or river or lake and grazed on the adjacent pasturelands during the course of the night:

> About fifty years ago in Faha there lived a man named Shaun Burns. He had a field of corn close to the shore and it was trespassed night after night. One night he stopped up watching it. He saw a multitude of grey horses coming in off the shore. He took up a lump of earth and threw it at the horses. He struck one grey mare. He brought her home and worked her for three years and she had three foals. He worked her away. One Sunday he tackled her. He left her standing in the yard and went in. She shook the tackling off herself and gave three neighs and called on her three foals and sped off towards the shore and was never heard of since.

A similar tale was told of far-famed Gleann na gCapall which nestles in the shadow of Mangerton mountain in Killarney. There were three lakes in Gleann na gCapall and there were three horses, one in each lake. One of the horses was snow white with a black blaze on his forehead; the second was jet black with a white star on his forehead; while the third was a magnificent bay with white spots on his forehead. Crops and gardens in the area were damaged and destroyed time and time again, and, at length, the tracks of horses were seen leading to the middle lake. Then one night a mare disappeared and thereafter a wise woman was consulted. She advised them to seek the help of a seventh son. Some nights later, he ordered all the people indoors, telling them to close all doors and windows and to extinguish all fires and lights. There was a violent storm that night, thunder rumbling through the heavens and fiery shafts of lightning raging down the night sky. There was frenzied galloping and neighing too, but next morning, to their surprise and delight, the people found that the missing mare had returned and that no further damage had been done to the crops during the course of the night. From that time onwards no tracks were ever traced leading in or out of the lake.

The fairies also had horses but like the horses that emerged from the sea theirs too were enchanted steeds:

Once upon a time there was a man and every night he used to go to the town. There was a forge on the side of the road. On his way home one night he met a large number of fairies at the forge and they were all riding on horseback. One of the fairies asked him would he go with them. He said he would if they gave him a horse. One of the fairies went in behind the forge and got an old plough that was thrown down on the ground. He changed it into a horse and told the man to get up on the horse's back but not to hit the horse. The man went up on his back and said he would not hit him, and off they went. The horse went off without a stop till they came to a big hedge. The horse would not jump it for him like all the other horses. Then he hit the horse and he changed it into a plough again and the man was left near the hedge till morning about a hundred miles from home.

In some folktales St Patrick had a snow white steed. On one occasion when he was given lodgings he told his hosts to put his horse in the stable and not to interfere with him. The people of the house recognised the saint and concluded that his horse was surely blessed, and that it might be no bad idea to ride the animal a few times round the farm during the course of the night. This they did. Next morning all the fields were like meadows and the trees were laden with blossoms and fruits. The householders contrived to keep the wonderful horse for themselves and gave St Patrick another. The saint had, however, travelled only a little distance along the road when he discovered his mistake. He returned to the house where he had spent the night and recovered his own horse, and for once he did not curse the inmates for the deception they had practised upon him.

Horses sometimes behaved oddly when passing a fort or a cemetery as this tale from County Cork illustrates:

A good many years ago there lived in Dangan a very old man whose name was Old Macanta. One day he fell suddenly ill and a neighbour who was called Mickleen Ruad was asked to go to Inch for the priest. He rode a white saddled horse and the priest rode another. The horse suddenly stopped when they were approaching Dangan churchyard. They did all that they could to make him go but the horse would not stir. At last the priest said that perhaps the dead wanted a song from Mickleen who had a beautiful voice. Mickleen said 'Maybe so', and with that he sang a fine song. When he had finished, both of them heard cheering and clapping of palms inside the fence. Then the priest said, 'As they liked it we'll give them another'. When he had finished there was double the cheering. When it ceased they heard the noise and the commotion going on in the direction of the burying ground. Then the horse trotted on better than ever.

There was also the tale of the ploughman who was sent by his master to plough a fort. The ploughman was very reluctant to enter the fort with his team of horses but the master told him that if he did not do so he would get no dinner. He harnessed the horses, and when he came to the fort he took off his cap and blessed himself. If anything dire happened it would not be his fault, he assured himself. He drove the horses into the fort and no sooner had he done so than he heard the sweetest music, whereupon the horses immediately began to dance for joy. The ploughman went to his employer and brought him to the fort, telling him what had happened. When the master set about ploughing, the music began again and the horses began to dance again. The master then decided to abandon his attempt to plough the fort.

Even more sinister was the tale of the smith who owned a forge near a fort. One night, about twelve o'clock, when he was working late in the forge a stranger in dark clothes came to the door and asked him if he would kindly put a shoe on his horse's foot. The smith was more than willing to do so, but seconds later the man returned not with a horse but with a horse's leg. The smith did the job, the man paid for the work and expressed his thanks, and seconds later the sound of galloping horse hoofs was heard echoing in the distance.

If foxes were seen on the occasion of a death at Gormanstown Castle then ghostly riders were very much in evidence following a death at Glin Castle. These riders apparently had lights on their helmets and spears in their hands. No sooner had the servants closed the castle gates but they were opened again. This happened time after time. The horses in the stables were untied too and joined in the mêlée.

Humour has always been a part of the Irish folk tradition, and that humour was sure to lift the spirits even more when it was at the expense of the local landlord. Such was the case of the youth who was about to sell his horse to the landlord. Now the landlord was an infamous miser and there was nothing he loved more than money, which was why his rents were the highest in the country. Jack, for that was the young man's name, had only one shilling left in the world, and he tossed the shilling into the horse's feed in the morning. Later, when the landlord saw that the horse passed the shilling, he offered Jack a great deal of money for him which Jack accepted without undue hesitation, having also received a written promise that henceforth he might have his holding completely free of rent.

Those who travelled about late at night often encountered withered old hags or ladies in white. The owner of a horse and cart might offer the hag or the lady in white a drive, but the horse generally died soon afterwards. This was not the case, however, in the tale of Control and Bought Sense:

John was returning home one evening and he was very satisfied with himself and his ounce of tobacco in his pocket. 'It is as well for me to hurry,' says he 'as my wife will be excited about me.' Just as he was about to cross a river, what stood before him but a big white spirit.

'Take me across the river,' said he, 'and I will give you power to understand the speech of the animals but for your life do not tell anyone the secret or if you do you will lose your gift.' He took the spirit over the river and went home. He went to the stable and gave some oats to the horses. One of them did not deserve the oats as he was in a stubborn fit all day and it was useless to try and make him work. He shut the door and listened to the horses: 'Yes,' said the disobedient horse, 'I have my share of oats like you who were working all day.' 'Yes', said the other horse, 'because our master is a fool.' On hearing this talk, the man burst out laughing and went in home

'Why were you laughing?' said his wife. He could not tell her for if he did he would give away his secret. The cause of the laughing was giving her so much trouble that she said she would die if he did not tell her.

'If that is so it is not my fault if you die.'

That remained as it was and he went to plough on the following day with the pair of horses, but the sulking horse would not stir. He put them in the stable and gave a big share of oats to the good horse and left the other with nothing. The result was that the sulking horse was dying with the hunger in a day or two. His wife was in bed pretending to be dying as she was not told the cause of the laughing.

On that evening he was again listening to the horses. 'Yes,' said the sulking horse, 'I am dying of famine.' 'You would not,' said the other 'if you worked as I did.' Then said the stubborn horse, 'Tomorrow is a long way off till I shall go working.' Then the man said in his own mind that the horse got sensible.

He turned to go in home but what was in the yard in front of him but a flock of geese with a gander in their midst and he beating his comrades as best he could. 'On my word,' said the gander to the geese. 'I will teach you sense and if that *pleidhce* [fool] does the same thing to his wife, I promise you that the lady will have a different tune to play.' When the man heard this he ran in home, seized his walking cane, went to where his wife was and threatened her with it.

'In the name of God,' she said at last, 'don't beat me or you'll be the worst off for it.' He went off the following day, ploughing, and I may say that the stubborn horse did the best work in spite of hunger and weakness and the man's wife was much more neat and kind from that on. The hungry horse got plenty of oats that evening, and indeed the two horses had a good feast. As regards John and his wife they were very kind to one another and they lived happily ever afterwards.

Curled horse hair was used in the filling of horse collars and saddles. It was of paramount importance that the filling for the collar should be curled and that these curls should remain in place. Otherwise the filling would be lumpy and uneven and would skin the horse. The hair was cut periodically from the mane and tail of the horse, and stored until sufficient had been accumulated. It was then washed and dried and twisted into a thin rope – less than half an inch in diameter. When the rope was about twelve to fifteen feet long it was formed into a ball of about four or five inches in diameter. Then a second ball was made, then a third and a fourth, and so until the required amount had been made. The balls of hair rope were hung from a rafter for about a month, after which they were placed in boiling water and allowed to boil for three or four hours. When thoroughly dry, the hair was teased out with the fingers, or combed so that literally every rib of curled hair was separated from its fellows.

The horse is very much a majestic animal and not surprisingly it figured in many tales of princes and kings:

Once there lived a king and queen and they had three handsome sons. The youngest was only three years when the queen died. Some years after, the king married a very wicked woman and she hated her stepsons. After a year a son was born to her and her hatred became more intense. She had a woman working in the palace who had a knowledge of witchcraft. One day the queen went to the woman's house and asked her how would she get rid of her stepsons. The woman gave her a pack of enchanted cards. One day she played a game with her stepsons, and whoever won should get their wish. The queen won two games and the youngest stepson won the last game. The queen wished that the three stepsons should get 'The White Steed of Bells' for her. Then the youngest stepson wished that she should stand on the top of the castle on the outside and live on bread and water until they would return.

One morning the three stepsons set off on their journey and after about a year wandering they met a man. The man told them that he was the Black Thief and he asked them what they were looking for. They told him they were looking for 'The White Steed of Bells', and he said that he knew where he was. They went on and the Black Thief went into a giant's house.

The giant was out and his wife told the thief that the giant had ordered a child killed for his dinner. She had a child at hand but the thief said it would be a good idea to give him an animal instead. She made the pie and put the animal's flesh into it. Then she cut the small finger off the child and put it on top of the pie. The giant came in and his wife gave him the pie and he said it tasted like animal's flesh, so she said it was not and she showed him the finger. He was satisfied then and the child was saved.

The Black Thief took away the child. Years after this, the three stepsons met the Black Thief again. Then they went to get the White Steed of Bells. When they came to the house where the White Steed was they went in, but they were caught by soldiers who were guarding the house. The four were to be put to death but the thief said if he told three good stories would they let the three stepsons go. He told the stories and they were left go. Then the judge said he was the only one to die himself. The thief told the story about the giant and how he had saved the child. Then he held up the left hand of the judge and he had no small finger. He was the man whom he had saved. The judge was delighted and he said he would give him anything he wished for. The thief wished for the White Steed of Bells and the judge gave it to him. The Black Thief gave the White Steed to the stepsons. Then the three stepsons took the White Steed of Bells home to the queen. When the queen saw them coming she threw herself off the top of the castle and she was killed. Then the three brothers got married and lived happily ever after.

If a horse was to be sold, his halter should never be sold with him. When a horse that had been sold for some time returned to the old owner's home, this was taken as a herald of death. One should never remove a horse's shoes when he was dead. He still had journeys to go. If a child had whooping cough one of the parents should keep travelling along the road until he or she met a man on a white horse – the parent should follow the rider's advice and this would cure the child. If you found a back tooth of a horse by chance and carried it about in your pocket you would never be short of money. It was considered unlucky to cross the path of a team of horses before the ploughman. Foals born at Whitsuntide would win races or kill men, but the best way to tame a horse was to whisper the creed into his right ear on Friday and his left ear on Wednesday. Dreams which featured horses were said to be very lucky, but misfortune would always ensue if a farmer violated the golden rule that one should never strike a horse with his own halter, and there were many salutary tales which told of the disasters that had befallen those who did so.

There were many old sayings about the horse. These included: 'A nod is as good as a wink to a blind horse'; 'Never look a gift horse in the mouth'; 'Live horse and you'll get grass'; and 'The borrowed horse has a hard hoof'. People were discouraged from being over zealous with the saying which reminded them that everyone laid a burden on the willing horse. Patience was recommended by another saying, 'Shabby colts make handsome horses', while if someone attempted something utterly futile he was reminded that one couldn't made a racehorse out of a jackass.

Horses were held to be sensitive animals and they were often acutely aware of sights and sounds of which their riders were ignorant. These ethereal phenomena very often had a malevolent aspect to them, and so the alertness of the horse saved its master from an encounter with mischievous fairies or spiteful demons. Some people had the evil eye, that is the power to overlook animals, and so if a farmer had a valuable horse or horses he took steps to ensure that his animals never came in contact with anyone reputed to possess the power of the evil eye, for if such a one held his gaze on an animal for a matter of seconds, the animal was doomed and nothing could save it. Others, however, possessed a more benign gift which in Irish speaking districts was known as *'cogar i gcluais capall'*. The one so blessed merely had to whisper in the ear of the most perverse, rebellious horse, and the horse became gentle and subdued in a matter of seconds. A great many travellers in particular were believed to have the gift of the *cogar* (whisper).

All over Ireland, however, there were people whose judgment in matters of the horse was widely acclaimed and respected. The following story is a good illustration: One day one of the servants came to Miss O'Sullivan in a great hurry and told her that the horses were killing themselves about a foal down near the river. A black mare and a foxy one were trying to take a foal off one another. The two mares had foaled that morning and one of the foals had died – a black foal with white legs from the knees down with a white blaze on the forehead. The foal that was still alive was foxy with a white star on its forehead. Tim Hartnett and the servant went in great haste to where the horses and the foals were and very soon a large crowd of people had gathered there. Soon Miss O'Sullivan arrived. She inspected the dead foal and the living foal and the two mares. 'A foal like each mare,' she concluded. She asked the vet (Tim Hartnett was known locally as the vet because he knew a great deal about animals) which mare gave birth to the living foal. He answered that the foxy mare was the mother of the foxy foal and the black mare was the mother of the black foal. She asked him was he sure and he said he was, as the living foal was the colour of the foxy mare. 'Oh,' said she, 'did you never see a black cow giving birth to a white calf? If as you say the foal is the same colour as the mare, that is no proof that she is her mother.' She asked all the people gathered round if they could prove which of the two mares had given birth to the living foal and they all had different opinions. 'I will prove it to ye in a few minutes,' said she 'which mare is the mother of the living foal.' She told one of the men to bring the foal to the bank of a river. The two mares followed. Then she told the man to ease the foal gently into the water. He did and immediately the black mare jumped in after her offspring. 'Well,' concluded Miss O'Sullivan, 'the black mare is the mother of the foal.' They all agreed that she was.

The seventh son possessed a charm for curing diseases in animals especially in horses and cattle. There was such a man named Dineen living in the Valley of Claodach which is near Glenflesk. It was said that he first discovered he had the charm when he went digging for worms for bait and found that when he touched the worms they died. A person born on Good Friday and baptised on Easter Sunday possessed similar powers.

Among the folk remedies used for treating horses was that of grounding the tops of Irish furze, *aitinn gaelach,* and mixing it with chopped mangolds or turnips. The mixture was recommended as a remedy for internal worms. Boiled turnips were also used in poultice form to reduce mild swellings in horses' legs and fetlocks. The roots of comfrey or thistles might also be boiled and applied in this way. Sometimes a horse might suffer from severe swelling in the hind legs. This condition was known as 'farcey' and there was at least one very colourful folk cure for it: The horse was taken to a man who was supposed to have a special charm, in this instance a man who had never seen his father. The owner of the horse was required to bring a pound of fresh butter with him. The man who had the charm sat on the horse's back and held the butter in his hands while he pronounced certain secret words. When the ceremony was complete he was allowed to keep the butter. Train oil and sulphur were used in the treating of mange and scruff.

If a horse suffered from gripe or colic he was walked fairly vigorously with a quilt or some such covering thrown over his back. A cure for glands in a horse's neck was to wash the neck with bluestone dissolved in hot water. Warts were generally removed with a pincers and the affected area cauterised. If a horse suffered from some malady in his lungs a large pot of hay was boiled and then transferred immediately to a small bag. A drop or two of eucalyptus oil was added to the hay and the bag was attached to the horse's head. The vapour from the bag was infused through the nostrils and apparently served to clear the lungs. The steaming bag of hay was placed about the horse's head three times a day. The bark of the oak boiled and applied to flesh wounds in a horse was held to be very effective.

The horse suffered from 'botts' when his stomach was infected with fleas or maggots. One treatment for this consisted of a mixture of linseed oil and a little turpentine. This was given to the animal two or three days in succession during which time the animal was made to fast.

* * *

The Donkey: The donkey is very much part of the Christmas story. The humble ass was said to have warmed the Christ Child on that first Christmas night in the stable in Bethlehem. The Virgin and Child travelled on the donkey's back during the Flight into Egypt, and ever since the donkey has a cross on its back. On Christmas night at midnight, all the animals in the world are given the power of speech and they all kneel down to pray in adoration of Christ. If a person had the good fortune to touch the cross on the donkey's back as it knelt and prayed on Christmas night then the nearest wish to their heart at that very moment would be granted. An Irish variation of the tale of the Flight into Egypt tells how at one time Our Lord was attempting to cross a river and he spied a mule in a field. He clambered on the mule's back but the mule reared on high and threw him to the ground. And then Our Lord said to the Mule, 'May you never have offspring.' Then he saw a donkey and the donkey gladly took him across the river. From that time onwards there was a cross on the donkey's back and he was the most blessed of animals. That is why too the shoe of a donkey always brings good luck.

The donkey, however, is much maligned in the old saying, 'As lazy as an ass.' It was said of someone who was light fingered that he would steal the cross off an ass' back. There was some good advice in the old proverb which asserted: 'Better the ass that carries you than the horse that throws you.' A person could be cured of the mumps if they wore a donkey's winkers and drank water from a well. If a child had whooping cough the treatment might involve the passing of the patient backwards and forwards over and under the body of an ass. The treatment was rendered more effective still if a strand of red string or red cloth were tied about the child's neck. A very wily saying about the donkey: 'The mule would be a horse but for his mother being an ass.'

Those who did not own horses were obliged to travel by donkey and cart. Here is an amusing story of one such traveller:

> There was a man living in Killahan named Thomas Halloran. One night he was going towards home with a donkey and cart and he had no light for his cart. He thought of a plan. He took the donkey out from under the cart and he pulled the cart along himself. He had to pass by the hut where the police lived in Killahan and as he was passing by, a policeman came out and asked for his light but the man told him to go back and ask the driver about it.

Patrick Kennedy gives the donkey a central role in his story of 'Jack and his Comrades':

> Once there was a poor widow, and often there was, and she had one son. A very lean summer came and they didn't know how they'd live till the new potatoes would be fit for eating. So Jack says to his mother one evening: 'Mother bake my cake and kill my cock till I go seek my fortune and if I meet it never fear but I'll be soon back to share it with you.' So she did as he asked her and he set off at the dawn of day on his journey. His mother

came along with him to the bawn gate and says she: 'Jack which would you rather have, half the cake and half the cock with my blessing or the whole of them with my curse?'

'O musha mother,' says Jack, 'why do you ask me that question? Since you know I wouldn't have your curse and Damer's estate along with it.'

'Well then, Jack,' says she, 'here's the whole lot of them and my thousand blessings with them.' So she stood at the bawn gate and blessed as far as her eyes could see him.

Well, he went along and along till he was tired and ne'er a farmer's house he went into wanted a boy. At last his road led by the side of a bog and there was a poor ass up to his shoulders near a big bunch of grass that he was trying to come at. 'Ah, then, Jack asthor,' says he, 'help me out or I'll be drownded.'

'Never sayt twice,' says Jack and he pitched in big stones and scraws into the slob till the ass got good ground under him.

'Thank you, Jack,' says he when he was out on the hard road. 'I'll do as much for you another time. Where are you going?'

'Faith, I'm gong to seek my fortune till harvest comes in, God bless it.'

'If you like,' says the ass, 'I'll go along with you. Who knows what luck we may strike?'

'With all my heart, It's getting late; let us be trotting.'

Well they were going through a village and a whole army of *garsúns* were hunting a poor dog with a kettle tied to his tail. He ran up to Jack for protection and the ass let such a roar out of him that the little thieves took to their heels as if the old boy was after them. 'More power to you, Jack,' says the dog. 'I'm much obliged to you. Where is the beast and yourself going?'

'We're going to seek our fortune till the harvest comes in.'

'And wouldn't I be proud to go with you,' says the dog, 'and get shut of them ill conducted boys. Purshuin to them.'

'Well, well, throw your tail over your arm and come along.'

They got outside the town and sat down under an old wall and Jack pulled out his bread and meat and shared with the dog, and the ass made his dinner on a bunch of thistles. While they were eating and chatting what should come by but a poor half starved cat and the meow he gave out of him would make your heart ache. 'You look as if you saw the tops of nine houses since breakfast,' says Jack. 'Here's a bone and something on it.'

'May your child never know a hungry belly,' says Tom. 'It's myself that's in need of your kindness. May I be so bold as to ax where ye are all going?'

'We're going to seek our fortune till the harvest comes in and you may join us if you like.'

'And that I'll do with a heart and a half,' says the cat, 'and thank you for axing me.'

Off they set again and just as the shadows of the trees were three times as long as themselves they heard a great crackling in the fields inside the road; and out over the ditch jumped a fox with a fine black cock in his mouth. 'Oh you anointed villain,' says the ass roaring like thunder.

'At him. Good dog,' says Jack, and the word wasn't out of his mouth when Collie was in full sweep after the *madra rua*. Reynard dropped his prize like a hot potato and was off like a shot and the poor cock came back fluttering and trembling to Jack and his comrades.

'Oh, musha neighbours,' says he. 'Wasn't it the height of luck that threw ye in my way. I won't forget yer kindness if ever I find you in hardship, and where in the world are ye all going?'

'We're going to seek our fortune till the harvest comes in; you may join our party if you like and sit on Neddy's crupper when your legs and wings are tired.

Well the march began again and just as the sun was going down they looked around and there was neither cabin nor farmhouse in sight. 'Well, well,' says Jack, 'the worse luck now the better another time and its only a summer night after all. We'll go into the wood and make our bed in the long grass.'

No sooner said than done. Jack stretched himself on a bunch of dry grass, the ass lay near him; the dog and the cat lay in the ass' warm lap and the cock went to roost in the next tree. Well the soundness of deep sleep was over them all when the cock took a notion of crowing. 'Bother you, *coileach dhubh* [black cock],' says the ass. 'You disturbed me from as nice a wisp of hay as ever I tasted. What's the matter?'

'It's daybreak, that's the matter. Don't you see the light yonder?'

'I see a light indeed,' says Jack, 'but it's from a candle it's coming and not from the sun. As you have roused us we may as well go over and ask for lodgings.'

So they all shook themselves and went on through grass and rocks and briars till they got down into a hollow and there was a light coming through the shadow and along with it came singing and laughing and cursing. 'Easy boys,' says Jack. 'Walk on your tippy toes till we see what sort of people we have to deal with.'

So they crept near the window and there they saw six robbers inside with pistols and blunderbusses and cutlasses, sitting at a table, eating roast beef and pork and drinking mulled beer and wine and whiskey punch.

'Wasn't that a fine haul we made at the Lord of Dunlavin's?' said one ugly thief and his mouth full. 'And it's little we'd get but for the honest porter. Here's his purty health.'

'The porter's purty health,' cried out every one of them and Jack bent his fingers at his comrades. 'Close your ranks, my men,' says he in a whisper, 'and let everyone mind the word of command.' So the ass put his forehoofs to the sill of the window; the dog got on the ass's head; the cat got on the dog's head and the cock on the cat's head. Then Jack made a sign and they all sang out like mad.

'Hee haw, hee haw,' roared the ass. 'Bow wow,' barked the dog. 'Meow, meow,' cried the cat. 'Cockadoodledoo,' shouted the cock.

'Level your pistols,' cried Jack, 'and make smithereens of them. Don't leave a mother's son of them alive. Present Fire.' With that they gave another haloo and smashed every pane in the window. The robbers were frightened out of their lives. They blew out the candles, threw down the table and skelped out the back door as if they were in earnest and never drew reign till they were in the very heart of the wood.

Jack and his party got into the room, closed the shutters, lighted the candles and ate and drank till hunger and thirst were gone. Then they lay down to rest; Jack in the bed, the ass in the stable, the dog on the doormat, the cat by the fire and the cock on the perch.

At first the robbers were very glad to find themselves safe in the thick wood but they soon began to get vexed. 'This damp grass is very different from our warm room,' says one.

'I was obliged to drop a fine crubeen,' says another.

'I didn't get a spoonful of my last tumbler,' says another.

'And all the Lord of Dunlavin's gold and silver that we left behind,' says the last.

'I think I'll venture back and see if I can recover anything,' says the captain.

'That's a good man,' says they all and off he went.

The lights were all out so he groped his way to the fire; and there the cat flew in his face and tore him with teeth and claws. He let a roar out of him and made for the room door to look for a candle inside. He trod on the dog's tail and if he did he got marks of teeth in his arms and legs and thighs. 'Mile murder,' cried he, 'I wish I was out of this unlucky house.' When he got to the exit door the cock dropped down on him with his claws and bill and what the cat and the dog done to him was only a bite to what he got from the cock. 'Oh tetterhation to ye all, ye unfeeling vagabones,' says he when he recovered his breath; and he staggered and spun round and round till he reeled into the stable, back first, but the ass received him with a kick in the broadest of his small clothes and landed him comfortably in the dunghill. When he came to himself he scratched his head and began to think what happened to him and as soon as he found that his legs were able to carry him he crawled away one foot after the other till he reached the wood.

'Well well,' cried they all, when he came within hearing,

'any chance of our property?'

'You may say chance,' says he, 'and itself is the poor chance all out. Ah, will any of ye pull a bed of grass for me? All the sticking plaster in Enniscorthy would be too little for the cuts and bruises I have on me. Ah, if you only knew what I have gone through for you. When I got to the kitchen fire looking for a sod of lighted turf, what should be there but a *cailleach* [hag] carding flax and you may see the marks she left on my face with the carders. I made to the room door as fast as I could and who should I stumble over but a cobbler and his seat and if he did not work at me with his awls and pincers you may call me a rogue. Well I got away from him somehow but when I was passing through the door it must have been the divil himself that pounced down on me with his claws and teeth that were equal to sixpenny nails and his wings – ill luck be on his road. Well at last I reached the stable and there by way of salute, I got a belt from a sledgehammer that sent me half a mile off. If you don't believe me you can go and judge for yourselves.'

'Oh my poor captain,' says they, 'we believe you to the mines. Catch us indeed going within a hen's race of that unlucky cabin.'

Well before the sun shook his doublet next morning, Jack and his comrades were up and about. They made a hearty breakfast on what was left the night before and then they all set off to the castle of the Lord of Dunlavin and gave back all his gold and silver. Jack put it all in the two ends of a sack and laid it across Neddy's back and all took the road in their hands. Away they went, through bogs, up hills, down dales and sometimes along the yalla high road till they came to the hall door of the Lord of Dunlavin and who should be there airing his powdered head, his white stockings and his red breeches but the thief of a porter. He gave a cross look to the visitors and says he to Jack: 'What do you want here my fine fellow? There isn't room for you all.'

'We want,' says Jack, 'what I'm sure you haven't to give us and that is common civility.'

'Come, be off, you lazy *geocachs*,' says he, 'while a cat id be licking her ear or I'll let the dogs at you.'

'Would you tell us,' says the cock that was perched on the ass's head 'who was it that opened the door for the robbers the other night?'

Ah maybe the porter's red face didn't turn the colour of his frill, and the Lord of Dunlavin and his pretty daughter that was standing at the parlour window, unbeknownst to the porter, put out their heads. 'I'd be glad, Barney,' says the master, 'to hear your answer to the gentleman with the red comb on him.'

'Ah my lord, don't believe the rascal. Sure I didn't open the door to them six robbers.'

'And how did you know there were six, you poor innocent?' says the Lord.

'Never mind, sir,' says Jack, 'all your gold and silver is there in that sack and I don't think you will begrudge us our supper and bed after our long walk from the wood of Athasach.'

'Begrudge indeed. Not one of you will ever see a poor day if I can help it.'

So all were welcomed to their hearts' content and the ass and the dog and the cock got the head jobs in the farmyard and the cat took possession of the kitchen. The lord took Jack in hand, dressed him in broadcloths and frills as white as snow and put a watch in his fob. When they sat down to dinner the lady of the house said that Jack had the air of a gentleman about him and the lord said he'd make him his steward. Jack brought his mother and settled her comfortably near the castle and all were as happy as you please. The old woman that told me the story said Jack and the young lady were married but if they were I hope he spent two or three years getting the education of a gentleman. I don't think that a country boy would feel comfortable striving to discourse for a well bred young lady, the length of a summer's day, even if he had the *Academy of Compliments* and the *Complete Letter Writer* by heart.

* * *

The Dog: It was believed that one should never ask a question of a dog for he had the capacity to answer, and if he chose to do so the one who posed the question would die in the near future. Dogs and cats were the most intelligent of all domestic animals; they listened to and understood everything that was said; they could interpret changes in facial expression in their human masters. If a dog howled near the sick room, there was very little hope that the patient would recover.

Dogs, like horses, were very susceptible to the influence of the fairies. However, when a dog saw a fairy or spirit it chose to howl rather than bark. The baying hound or the *gaidhrín caointeach* sometimes took the place of the banshee and was heard before a death in certain families.

Fairy or phantom animals figure prominently in Irish folklore. There were numerous tales which described sightings of phantom dogs. These dogs were generally large and black and vicious and were usually seen by those who stayed out too late at night. Some phantom dogs, however, possessed the capacity to change both their size and their colour at will. The Black Woolly Dog is the story of an enchanted dog, but the dog in this instance is not a malevolent creature:

There was once a gentleman who had three daughters. He also had a special chair and no one was allowed to sit in it. One day when he was out, the youngest daughter sat in the chair and made a wish. A black woolly dog came and stood before her. Her two sisters then sat on the chair in turn and made a wish that they might each have a handsome gentleman. Their wish was granted. They all got married, the youngest daughter to the black woolly dog, and then they all left home with their husbands.

They came back (to their parents' house) after a year. Each couple had a child. The black woolly dog's wife came in a fine carriage and the black woolly dog running along the road by the side of it. After supper and when all was over they went to bed. The girls' mother went to see how they were situated. She saw that the black woolly dog was a handsome young man and there was an enchanted cap beside his head in the bed. The mother wanted to burn the cap but her husband argued against it. The three couples departed the following day and returned the following year, each couple now having two children each. It happened as before. The mother went to see how they were situated and she noticed the cap. She wished to burn it but again her husband intervened. After the third year the three couples came back again with three children each. The mother came to see how they were situated. This time she took the cap from the bed and threw it into the fire. The young man heard it and told his wife he would have to leave her now that the enchanted cap had been burned.

Next morning he set out on his journey but his wife followed him. The young man advised her to return to her parents; she would see no more of himself, and yet she continued to follow him. It was getting late and he directed her to a house telling her to seek lodgings there and if there was any difficulty to ask for the lodgings in the name of the black woolly dog. After supper she went to bed while the old woman who owned the house took care of the eldest child. She pulled out the fire and put him behind it but he leapt out again. 'True it is,' said she, 'you are a son of the black woolly dog.' When the young woman was leaving the next morning the owner of the house presented her with a bowl that would always be filled with food and drink whenever she felt hungry and thirsty.

She followed her husband throughout the next day and again at nightfall he directed her to a house where she would get lodgings. After supper she went to bed and the old woman put the second child behind the fire but he leapt out. 'True it is,' said she. 'You are a son of the black woolly dog.' When the young woman was leaving she was given a scissors by the old woman who said that if she cut a torn dress with it she would have a splendid suit of silk.

She followed her husband throughout the third day. Night came again and he directed her to a house where she would find lodgings. After supper she went to bed. The fire was pulled out; the third child was put behind it but he leapt out. The old woman said, 'It is true. You are a son of the black woolly dog.' On leaving, the young woman got a comb which would give her a beautiful head of hair every time she combed her hair.

She followed her husband throughout the next day. She kept close to him until he pulled a rush and went down through the earth. She grabbed at his hair and pulled away a rib. A drop of blood fell on his shirt. She began to dig up the ground where the husband had vanished. When night came she clambered high into a tree to rest. There was a spring well near the tree. A servant girl from a nearby house came to the well for water. The moon was shining and the night was bright. The servant girl saw the shadow of the woman in the well and dropped the bucket. The blacksmith who owned the house came to the well himself and he discovered the woman in the tree. He took her to his house and both himself and his wife treated her with kindness. They noticed that her fingernails were broken from digging the ground, so the blacksmith made and fitted steel nails for her fingers.

She spent a year digging up the ground. Then one day as she sat on a riverbank she heard a girl crying as she was washing. The woman asked her what was the matter. The servant replied that there was a bloodstain on her master's shirt and that no one could remove it but his lawful wife. The woman rubbed the shirt and the bloodstain disappeared. When the servant girl returned to her work underground the old witch who was at this time married to the black woolly dog came to know that his lawful wife was near at hand and that she had in her possession three enchanted things – a bowl, a scissors and a comb. She asked the servant to ask if the woman would part with the bowl and if so what she desired in return. The woman said that she would give the bowl to the witch if she could spend a night in bed with her husband. The witch agreed but she gave the black woolly dog a sleeping draught so that when the time came he did not even know that his lawful wife was with him. The same thing happened the second time but then the black woolly dog came to hear that his young wife had been with him and that he had been unaware of it. This time the servant girl contrived to spill the sleeping draught. His lawful wife came to the black woolly dog but the witch screamed with rage, vowing that she would have nothing more to do with him and that she would have her revenge. A servant boy, however, killed the witch by stabbing her in the eye with a blazing spear. The black woolly dog and his wife lived happily ever after.

There were many tales of faithful dogs who had strayed at a fair or market but still found their way home miles and miles away. Some dogs travelled extraordinary distances on such occasions. Here is a tale which illustrates the intelligence of man's best friend:

> At one time there was a match between Ardea and Douros. In the *sliabh* [mountain] near Clonee Bridge they played it. Very often the ball was kicked out into the lake and when this happened the dog always swam out after it without anyone telling him to do so. One time his owner missed a horse that they had bought from a man who lived near Cloherane. The horse had left Ardea during the night and had reached Cloherane the next day. The people searched and searched for the animal. At length, they told the dog to go and find him. The dog, accompanied by some of the family set out on his journey and he never came to a stop till he reached Cloherane mountain. There, high up on the mountain, he came upon the horse and drove her down. It was his custom to meet the horse and cart coming from town and he could always distinguish it from other horses and carts. One night one of the boys lost a rug from the cart, but the dog was behind the cart and brought the rug home with him in his mouth. He lived to a good old age of fourteen and his name was Shep.

When a dog ate grass he was said to be taking his medicine. Train oil and sulphur were used for treating mange in dogs. There was an unusual cure for dogs that were prone to fits of one kind or another. The owner took some blue that was used in the washing of clothes and mixed it with a little blue stone (copper sulphate). Water was then added and the solution given as a tonic three times a day to the dog. An alternative approach was to boil garlic in new milk which was then given to the patient. Milk and cod liver oil was yet another remedy for a dog susceptible to fits. If this concoction seemed too revolting, then he might be washed in a tub of cold water, and paraffin oil poured into his ears. It was believed that if a dog ate too much red meat he might develop distemper. An application of strong cold tea to the eyes was sometimes recommended for dogs suffering from distemper, while forge water was considered very effective in the treatment of ring worm in dogs and other animals. Sometimes heather was boiled in water and then strained, the resulting heather water being considered to have certain curative properties which helped to maintain man's best friend in good condition. The touch from the hand of a seventh son cured the bite of a mad dog.

There were several old sayings involving the dog, amongst them the following: 'Hold onto the bone and the dog will follow you'; 'Let sleeping dogs lie'; 'Run with the hare and hunt with the hounds'; 'Little dogs start the hare but great dogs catch her'; 'If you lie down with dogs you'll rise with fleas'; 'A great barker seldom bites'; 'You can't teach an old dog new tricks'; 'Every dog is a brave soldier on his own doorstep'; 'It is a bad dog that is not worth the whistling'; 'Better to have the dog's welcome than his bite'; 'The old dog for the hard road'; 'The old dog sleeps near the fire but he doesn't burn himself'; and 'The dog that buries his bones is either well fed or well advised.' (As the owner of a black labrador that has a great penchant for burying his bones, I sometimes think he is both well fed and well advised.)

It was widely believed in Kerry that one should never say 'God Bless it' of a dog. The tradition arose from the tale of a Kerry priest who, while on his way to the home of a dying man, heard a sweet voice singing the old favourite, 'Cailín Deas Cruite na mBó'. The priest lingered and listened for it was the most mellifluous rendition of the song he had ever heard. The listener became more and more curious. It was a great wonder that the owner of that beautiful voice had not come to his attention before for he was known throughout the length and breadth of the parish as a lover of music and song. Forgetting his errand for a few moments, the priest clambered into a nearby field to see if he could catch a glimpse of the sweet throated songster, when what should he see before him but a demon dog singing to his heart's content. It was only then that the priest recollected the urgency with which he had been summoned to the home of the dying man, but when he reached the house the man was dead for he had been listening to the dog much longer than he had at first imagined. The priest was filled with remorse and vowed that henceforth no one should ever say 'God Bless it' of a dog again. In some versions of the story, however, the cat and not the dog was the villain of the piece.

A tale was told in *Bealoideas* of the beggar who came looking for shelter. The woman of the house said he was welcome to take shelter. He found a bean in the yard and gave it to the good woman for safekeeping. The bean was eaten by a hen; the beggar claimed the hen. The hen was eaten by a sow; he claimed the sow; the sow was killed by a horse; he claimed the horse; he asked the woman to send her daughter to mind the horse but the horse leapt over a cliff and the beggar claimed the daughter. The beggar placed the girl in a big bag but when his back was turned the woman of the house set the daughter free and put a dog, Bully Mór Bán, in her place. Later when the beggar had travelled a considerable distance he opened the bag. The dog jumped out and ran off, with the bag hanging to him – thus the beggar was left without bean or hen, sow or horse, girl or dog or bag.

* * *

The Pig: Why the priest and the pig should be associated in proverbs is a matter of conjecture, but they were associated in at least two old sayings. One proclaimed: 'The priest's pig gets the most porridge', while another contained this little gem of Irish wisdom: 'The priest that's a pet and the pig that's a pet are the two worst pets of all.'

The pig and the pigsty featured in a number of old folk beliefs. If a child had the mumps he might be taken to the pigsty where his head was then rubbed to the pig's back and prayers said, the hope being that the sickness would transfer from the child to the animal. Sometimes an incantation such as '*Muc, muc seo chughat an leicneach*' (Pig, pig, here are the mumps for you) was used on such occasions.

If one wished ill luck on one's neighbours the best method of placing a curse on him was that of burying a dead animal on his property. If no dead animal could be found, rotten eggs might prove to be a useful substitute. The custom is described very vividly in the following tale:

Long ago the old people were supposed to turn bad luck over on their neighbours. If their cattle died they buried the dead animal in their neighbour's boundary fence unknownst to him. When they did this the neighbour's cattle were supposed to die instead. A certain farmer in Lixnaw had no luck with his pigs no matter how he cared for them. One day the farmer and his servant were fencing the boundary ditch and they found a pig's carcass buried in it. They had a certain farmer's wife down for it – the *piseog* [superstition]. The woman one day met the above farmer's daughter on the road; she gave her a dead bonham inside in a paper sugar bag with instructions to throw the parcel into the river on the way home. This canal was bounding both farms. When the little girl left the woman she opened the parcel and found the dead bonham. Being innocent of the woman's wiles, she threw the parcel into the river. She told the story on arriving home and the farmer told the priest. The priest gave the farmer medals to bury in every field and to put in the outhouses. He also blessed the outhouses and better luck came to the farmer.

If someone wished ill luck on his neighbour's animals, he might make a small wax model of the neighbour in question, stick pins in it and toss it in cavalier fashion into the field.

Blood was always shed on St Martin's Eve. Very often a cock was killed, but in many parts it was a hapless pig that was led to the slaughter. Dire consequences would befall those who chose to ignore this time honoured ritual.

A labourer named Paddy Sullivan lived in Caherula about fifty years ago. On one occasion he got a pet bonham from a local farmer. The bonham throve with him and after a few months she had grown into a fine fat *céis* [young pig]. Paddy watched with satisfaction his pig increasing in weight and he thought of the way she would make a few pounds for him. But alas one morning when he went to the sty with her breakfast he found her very ill indeed. After trying several remedies recommended to him he found that the pig was daily getting worse and worse. One day a neighbour told him to promise St Martin that he would kill the pig in his honour on 10 November. He did so and the pig got as well as ever in the course of a few days. The pig increased in weight and about a fortnight before St Martin's Eve he decided to sell it at the Tralee pig fair. He left home for the fair before daylight. A neighbour who knew of the promise he had made to St Martin went inside the ditch beside the road and shouted out several times: 'Give the pig to Saint Martin! Give the pig to Saint Martin!' Sullivan got afraid, returned home and when St Martin's Eve came he killed the pig and had plenty of bacon for the winter.

Another widespread superstition is illustrated in this tale of the yank and the pigs:

Paddy the yank had very hard luck with his pigs long years ago. All his sows died and according as he'd buy a young sow or a litter of bonhams they would die. A neighbour of his, a very knowledgeable old woman, Tom Daly's mother, sent for him one night when she heard he was about buying another supply of bonhams. When he arrived she said to him, 'Don't go to the fair tomorrow. Wait until I send you some money to help you buy them.'

'All right,' said Paddy. About a month later, the night before the next fair, Nell came over to Connors. She gave Paddy the money. He went to the fair next day and bought the bonhams and every one of them lived and thrived. Nell told him that that was egg money she gave him and that egg money was always lucky.

There was an old custom that when a sow had bonhams she should be brought into the kitchen with her young and left there for ten days and nine nights. Fairy pigs were by no means as numerous as phantom dogs and demon cats but they were not unknown. There was one salutary tale of a man whose clock stopped and who set out for the fair in the middle of the night in his ass and cart. He had not travelled far when he met a fairy pig , and the brazen pig not only followed him, but even tried to get into the cart. A little further on was a bridge over a little stream, and the driver was confident that he would make his escape at the bridge for, as is well known, a fairy of any kind, whether he is a pig or not, cannot cross over water. When they came to the bridge the pig had to undertake a detour through the fields but, as chance would have it, one of the wheels fell off the cart – but then maybe it was not chance at all but the malevolent influence of that petulant pig. When the wheel had been re-fitted the pig came dashing airily through the fields and pursued the ass and cart once more. The driver was so terrified that he screamed at the owner of a house beside the road to open the door for him. The kind householder, being a most obliging sort, did as he was asked, whereupon the driver gave an athletic leap across a high stone wall and hurried indoors. The fairy pig was suitably disgruntled and vented his frustration by roaring and grunting outside the bedroom window for the remainder of the night. Some pigs just never give up, do they?

Pigs were often seen going in and out of forts, which would seem to indicate that the fairies were as fond of their bacon and cabbage as their human neighbours. Occasionally, pigs came out of rivers and streams, and these too were enchanted porkers. It was held to be unlucky to kill a pig on Monday. There was another tradition which proclaimed that the sow always had trouble giving birth because a pig put sods on our Lord's grave.

Among the most popular old sayings which feature the pig was one which cautioned: 'Don't give cherries to a pig; don't give advice to a fool.' An equally cynical view of the world was expressed in the proverb: 'The Miller's pigs are fat but God only knows whose meal they ate.' If a person was financially secure, or 'comfortably off' to use the country expression, he was said to be 'lying in lavender like Paddy's pig'. There was some good advice too for the indolent: 'A man without initiative is no better than a pig', but attempting the impossible would bring no rewards: 'You can't make a silk purse out of sow's ear.'

Caisearbháin [Dandelions] and nettles were often fed to pigs. The roots of comfrey, when boiled and mixed with the pig's meal, provided an effective cure for swine fever. Those who lived near the sea might wash their pigs with sea water if their porkers suffered from cramps. The story of 'Gallows Green' was a favourite pig story and, though there might be many slight variations, the basic theme was still the same.:

In olden times there lived a rich man who had only one son whose name was Jack. In those days there were poor scholars going from house to house teaching, as there were no national schools. A wandering scholar came to this man's house to teach Jack. He was fifteen years old when he had him taught. When he was leaving he wrote a note and put it in a locket and told him not to open the locket or read the note until he would be twenty-one years. He was in trouble day after day. When he was eighteen years he opened the locket and read the contents. What was written on the note was 'Gallows Green will be your end'. He did not care what he would do from that out. He thought he would be hanged. He left his father's house and went away into a big city. He worked with a cooper there for his board and lodgings. The Mayor of the town had a pig and it was the custom that every householder should give the pig a free dinner in his turn. It happened that the pig came to the cooper's house for his dinner one day. Jack said to the cooper: 'You have a fine pig,'

'He's not mine,' said the cooper. 'He's belonging to the Mayor of the town.'

'He's ours now,' said Jack getting the hatchet and killing the pig.

The mayor of the town missed the pig and sent out a soldier who should get a free meal every day and the soldier would know the taste of the Mayor's pig. The soldier went into the cooper's house one day and asked for his dinner. Jack said to him: 'I will give you a good feed of the Mayor's pig.' When the soldier had finished his dinner Jack hit him a stroke of a hatchet and killed him. Jack said to the cooper: 'Get ready. We must bury the soldier. We do not want him here.'

The mayor was planning how he would catch the thief. He had a big shed with an open front so he ranged barrels and filled them with tar and he filled the shed with gold. Jack spied the shed of gold when he was walking the street and he said to the cooper: 'We will go tonight for a bag of gold.' Both of them went, and Jack raised the cooper across the tar barrels and told him to fill the bag of gold and give it out to him. He reached out the bag of gold to Jack, but when he was coming out he staggered and fell into a barrel of tar and there was nothing exposed but his head. Jack did his best to pull him out but he couldn't so he cut off the head and carried it home by the whiskers.

The mayor thought of another plan. He put on a big dance for the poor and for the rich of the town. He put his daughter into a separate room. She was a fine looking lady, and the Mayor thought that the thief would surely try to steal the daughter. Jack went into the room and fell in love with her. The Mayor and the soldiers arrested him and he owned up to everything he had done. 'First I killed your pig; second I killed your soldier; third I stole your gold, fourth I killed the cooper and fifth I'm in love with your daughter.' Gallose Green was her name. They got married and lived happily ever after.

'Wat Wat' was the expression used when calling the pigs, but what would happen if the pigs called back? Here is a salutary tale of the servant girl and the speaking sow:

A servant girl was working in a farmer's house in Currans. The sow had bonhams and the girl had to stay up all night minding them. She had nothing to do, so she made bread and she put it on the griddle and soon she heard a loud voice saying: 'Mary O'Sullivan, your cake is burning.' She looked around and saw nobody. She ran to the woman of the house and said to her: 'I will stay here no longer.' So she went away. After a time she went across to America. A week afterwards she died and was never heard of again.

Here is a more amusing tale:

Three labourers had been employed by a farmer. The farmer also kept a servant boy. One day as the four went in to dinner to the farmer's house, one of the labourers noticed that the servant boy was not eating the meat which was prepared for them. He asked the servant boy why wasn't he eating the meat. The servant boy said it was the meat of an old boar. Any of them were not eating the meat on the following day and the farmer asked them why weren't they taking their dinner. One of the men being a poet answered him in rhyme:

> 'O Lord on high that rules the sky
> Look down upon us four.

And give us meat that we can eat
And take away this boar.'

* * *

Cats: In olden times when a visitor came to a house he might say, 'God bless all here except the cat', which would seem to illustrate that cats were held in something less than affection. Cats were mysterious creatures and were sometimes believed to be manifestations of evil, even of the devil himself. The familiars of witches have invariably been cats. For instance Dame Alice Kytler, a celebrated fourteenth-century witch of Kilkenny, was said to have had a demon lover who came to her in a number of guises, but most frequently in the guise of a cat. Much later, in the eighteenth century, in the tale of the witches of Island Magee, one of the principal characters, Mrs Hattridge, was sitting by the fire when a strange apparition came to her in the form of a boy. He held a book in his hands and, when asked if he could read, he blithely retorted that he had been taught to do so by the devil. A servant appeared on the scene and locked the door, but the wily intruder was not in the least impressed for he could come and go through the smallest space in the shape of a cat or mouse.

It was perhaps inevitable that the cat, because of its reserved and independent nature, should be regarded with some mistrust. Cats, it was believed, had the power not only to understand human speech but also to speak themselves when it seemed judicious to do so. One of the most popular tales in Irish folklore was of the cat who asked for a pair of shoes. Here is just one version:

Once upon a time there lived a very old man named Wat. He had three or four children. One night he was sitting around the fire with them and was saying that he should bring one of them a pair of shoes. The cat was listening too and she said to him: 'What about me Wat?'

'Oh,' says he, 'I'll bring you a pair of shoes too but I must get a pair for my children first.'

He went to town the next day for the shoes for his children, and he told the man of the hounds about the cat, and to meet him at a certain place when he was bringing the cat. So this day he went to town with the cat inside in the bag to measure the shoes. When he came near this place, the cat heard the hounds and she told Wat to mind her from them.

'Stay where you are and you will be safe,' said Wat. When the hounds came near he caught the cat and the bag and flung them out on the road. The dogs chased her and when she was going away the cat said: 'Ah, 'tis well for you, Wat. If I caught you I would choke you.'

Another story to illustrate why humans can never trust a cat:

In the townland of Glenderry very near our school there lived a woman named Biddy Grady. She was married to a man named Paddy Gloster and they lived about fifty years ago in this district. She had two sons whose names were Paddy Gloster and Johnny Gloster. Their father was dead and the two sons were earning their hire every day. They came home every Saturday evening as their mother was alone. She had a big black cat. There was a small little shop next door, owned by a person named Mary Dowling and she sold fish. It happened this night, however, that the two sons were coming home. Their mother always had a supper ready for them; it consisted of potatoes and fish, and meat was unheard of by the people in those days. This night she had no fish so she said to the cat: 'We have no fish tonight for my son's supper.'

'You won't be long with that story,' said the cat and he went out the door. He was not long outside when she heard him coming in and he had two herrings and a mackerel in his mouth and he gave them to the woman to put them into a pot over the fire to boil. The two sons came in and she told them the story. They put the black cat under a pot to smother him. When he was nearly dead he said, 'It was good for you that you put me here because otherwise you would not be alive tonight.'

The cat was a great pet by her so she was surprised when she heard him talking back to her. It frightened her very much for it was not a natural thing for a cat to do. I suppose but for the sons coming home he would have brought all the cats in the neighbourhood to put her to death. From this we learn that no matter how friendly you are with a cat you can never trust him.

Sometimes the cat came back to try and wreak vengeance on his aggressors as is the case of the talking cat who asked for a piece of turkey at supper time. He was given a piece of the turkey but was soon deposited in a bag, carried out to sea in a boat and promptly tossed overboard. He escaped from the bag and swam back to the shore. The tale has a rather gruesome end, for when the cat returned, the man of the house trapped his head between the door and the frame. A servant boy was called upon to find a hatchet and cut off the offending head. When the dripping head had almost been completely severed it declared vindictively that only their prompt action had saved them all from certain death.

You might rid yourself of a demon cat who came to steal your fish, by sprinkling him with holy water. When a woman in Connemara was thus afflicted she sprinkled the great black cat with holy water. Very soon the kitchen was filled with dense black smoke, through which nothing could be seen save the two red eyes of the cat blazing like coals of fire. All the while there was a strong smell of burning, but at length the smoke disappeared and the housewife discovered that the body of the demon cat had burned to cinders.

Another favourite theme concerning cats in Irish folklore was that the king of the cats was dead. The basic story was always the same despite minor variations in embellishment from place to place.

> Long ago there was a man coming from the fair. It was very late and he had to cross a wood. He met a leprechaun. He asked the leprechaun would he take a smoke and he said no, but he said 'you are very generous.' The leprechaun had a sword in his hand. He gave him the sword to protect him from the wild cats. As he was going home he saw all the wild cats. They went up on the horse's back and as they were going up he killed them one by one. The last was a big black cat. When he jumped up the man struck him with the sword. He fell to the ground and when he was dying he said to the man: 'When you go home tell Wauteer that you killed the king of the cats and no more cats will attack you.' The man went home and he was telling the story to his wife. The cat in the corner was listening. He leapt up against the man's throat and stuck his claws into it. He would have him killed only his wife killed the cat with the sword he got from the leprechaun.

Many country people were afraid to glance at a cat that had just washed its face, for the first person the cat cast his gaze upon after the washing, was doomed to die. Another superstition recommended that a cat should never be allowed into a new house until a year had elapsed. When people were moving to a new house the cat should be left behind. If this were not done the cat would start talking at twelve o'clock each night in the new house. However, if a black cat came into a house on Christmas night, the people of the house would have great luck throughout the year that followed. A purring cat or a cat with its back to the fire implied that rain was on the way. If a cat captured a mouse and allowed it to escape for no apparent reason this was taken as an omen of bad luck.

The blood of a black cat might be used to treat St Anthony's fire. If the liver of a black cat was ground into a fine powder and infused into a potion it served as a powerful aphrodisiac. The one who drank the potion would instantly fall passionately in love with the one who proffered it. The tale was told of the pretty Nora who wooed the young squire with a potent brew of strong tea laced with the ground liver of a cat. The squire inevitably fell head over heels in love with the coquettish Nora and made a proposal of marriage to her, but he was saved from a fate worse than death when some of his relatives set upon him with hazel sticks in the most vigorous manner possible. He was dragged from the bosom of his betrothed on the eve of their wedding night. He soon recovered, however, for the power of the hazel sticks had overcome the influence of Nora's sorcery – and if the squire complained of a sore head for a few weeks, well at least he had been spared the indignity of spending the rest of his life with one who enjoyed killing cats and pulverising their livers.

Not all cats were malevolent:

An old woman sat up very late spinning when a knocking came to her door. 'Who's there?' she asked. No answer but still the knocking went on. 'Who is there?' she asked a second time. Still no answer and the knocking continued. 'Who is there?' she asked the third time in a very angry passion.

Then came a small voice: 'Ah Judy, *a ghrá*, let me in for I am cold and hungry. Open the door, Judy *a ghrá*, and let me sit by the fire for the night is cold out here. Judy *a ghrá*, let me in, let me in.'

The heart of Judy was touched for she thought that it was some small child that had lost its way, and she rose up from her spinning and went and opened the door – when in walked a large black cat with a white breast, and two kittens after her. They all made over to the fire and began to warm and dry themselves, purring all the time very loudly, but Judy said never a word, only went on spinning. Then the black cat spoke at last: 'Judy *a ghrá*, don't stay up so late again for the fairies wanted to hold a council here tonight and to have some supper but you have prevented them, so they were very angry and determined to kill you, and only for myself and my two daughters here you would have been dead by this time. So take my advice. Don't interfere with the fairy hours again, for the night is their's and they hate to look upon the face of a mortal when they are out for pleasure or business. So I ran on to tell you, and now give me a drink of milk for I must be off.' After the milk was finished the cat stood up and called her daughters to come away. 'Good night, Judy, *a ghrá*,' she said. 'You have been civil to me and I'll not forget it. Good night. Good night.' With that, the black and the two kittens whisked up the chimney, but Judy looking down saw something glittering in the hearth and, taking it up, she found it was a piece of silver, more than she ever could make in a month by her spinning and she never again sat up so late to interfere with the fairy hours, but the black cat and her daughters came no more again to the house.

Those who were constantly quarrelling were said to fight like Kilkenny cats. The cat's fondness for cream was well encapsulated in the proverb: 'If the cat had a churn she would never take her paw from it.' Of a cunning woman it might be said: 'She would drink the cream and say her cat was a rogue.' Self interest was very much part of the character of the cat: 'The cat is her own best adviser', 'It's for her own good that the cat purrs' and 'An old cat will not burn herself'. If you were rebuked for your audacity you might retort, 'The cat can look at the queen.' The most popular saying concerning the cat was: 'Nature breaks out through the eyes of the cat', a similar theme being expressed in the proverb: 'What can the cat do but kill mice?'

One very popular folktale in rural Ireland was called 'Belling the Cat'. This tale warned its listeners of the folly of attempting the impossible:

There were these mice in a house one time and they had a great time of it till the man of the house brought home a big black cat from the fair one day Then the mice had the *ruaille buaille* [commotion] for they couldn't put their snouts beyond the skirting board but the cat was after them. Oh, the cat was a right villain – he gave the poor mice no peace. So one night when the cat had gone to bed the mice held a big confab about what was to be done with the divil of a cat. After a while one of the younger mice said: 'We'll tie a bell round the cat's neck and that will put a stop to his antics, for every time we hear the bell ringing won't we know the cat is at hand.' Well, there was great clapping, for it was a grand idea entirely, they all said, and they were slapping the young mouse on the back telling him he was the soundest mouse in the country.

Then a very old feeble mouse with grey hair that had kept quiet in a corner spoke up. 'Tell me now,' says he, 'which wan of ye fine fellows is volunteerin' to put the bell on the cat's neck, for that's the crux of the matter isn't it?' The gathering fell silent and the mice looked from one to the other hoping that some poor fool of a hero might volunteer to bell the cat, but there were no fools and no volunteers. After that there was no talk of belling the cat.

People who boasted of impractical plans and schemes were said to be 'belling the cat'.

Another of my favourite stories concerning the cat is this little one which describes his three blessings:

> Long ago there was a cat and he was a poor honest craythur. He had only three half pennies in the entire world but he put them to good use. He gave the first half penny for the forgetfulness of the housewife so that she might forget to store away the cream and the butter and the fish; he gave the second half penny so that he might be able to see in the night; and the third half penny that he might always have a warm comfortable bed beside the fire. Didn't he put his half pennies to good use and wasn't it he had the sense? The cat has those three blessings ever since.

* * *

Cows: The cow was perhaps the most important animal on the farm, and, not surprisingly, it was surrounded by a great wealth of folk tradition. One of the loveliest traditions was that of giving each individual cow a name. Very often they were named after their former owners such as Palmer and Red Hanlon, sometimes their name derived from their colour or from some distinctive marking such as Bawney and Spotty; occasionally they might be named after some personality trait or habit, such as Jumper or Kicker.

It was thought very important to protect the cow house from evil influences, and this could be done in a number of ways. A horse shoe, a piece of coloured wool, or a piece of oak – *rath doire* – might be kept hanging on the walls of the cowhouse for luck. Another favourite was the St Brigid's cross. Sometimes the old rushwork cross was removed and the new one put in place, but sometimes they were allowed to accumulate down through the years. Less common was the practice of adorning the walls with the shells of eggs that had hatched, while in some areas garlic was grown in a pot to ensure that the cows remained healthy. Very often when a cow or calf died one of his legs was hung in the cowhouse so that the remainder of the stock would enjoy good health and good fortune. Pictures of the Saviour and of the Blessed Virgin were also to be seen gracing the walls of the byre. Sometimes the oldest cow was milked first, and it was considered a very bad omen if some of the milk was spilled during milking. Very often the milker sang a song:

> The old women always sang a song when milking and some do it still. The cow gives her milk more freely and I have known an instance where the cow refused to give her milk because it was a stranger who milked her but when that stranger began to sing the cow then gave her milk freely.

There were many traditions associated with May Day in Ireland and many of these centred on the protection of cattle from evil influences. On May Day no householder would give away milk, water, salt or *gríosach*, the latter being a coal to redden the fire. If milk or butter was given away that day, the luck of the dairy for the year that followed would go with it:

> If anyone came to the house for milk on May Day, especially one who was known to have plenty of milk at home, it was thought they could take away the luck of the produce of the milk by charm. If butter were given away on the same day he who gave it would not make butter during that year even if he were churning from dawn till dark.

Even if a spancel were stolen on May Eve or May Day the luck of the cow would go with it, which served to explain why cattle were carefully watched about this time. The working of the churn could also be protected in a number of ways – either by nailing a horseshoe to the bottom of the churn or by placing a coal of fire and some salt beneath the churn. The most popular method of protecting the churn, however, was to encircle it with a garland of mountain ash. In some areas it was also believed that if a branch of mountain ash were woven into the ceiling, the house would have luck for the year that followed, while a boat that incorporated even the smallest amount of mountain ash in its construction would never be upset in a storm. Small crosses of rowan tree were sometimes fastened to the cows' tails on May Day. If anyone came to the house while the churning was in progress, he or she was required to take a hand at the churn if only for a few moments. Sometimes, cattle, especially cattle that were unwell, might be driven into a fort during the night in the hope that they might be restored to health. While it was forbidden to give away milk on May Day, nevertheless it was thought prudent to spill milk on the threshold to prevent evil spirits and fairies from gaining access to the household. Water from wells, especially holy wells, was particularly potent at this time of the year. Sir William Wilde wrote:

> Do not all these observances with respect to cows and all these

precautions relating to butter and milk go some way to establish the fact of the primitive Irish being a pastoral and cattle feeding people?

Strangers were especially suspect but if a snow-white heifer appeared among the cattle, this was said to bring the farmer the best of good luck during the year that followed.

> She goes with the sun and he forgets to burn,
> And the moon turns his face with love to her,
> My fair white cow of the mountain.

Hags who had turned themselves into hares were particularly active on May morning, when their chief occupation was that of milking unsuspecting cows, which allowed them to bewitch the produce of such cows:

> On May Day if they can find a hare among their herd, they endeavour to kill it, out of a notion that it is some old witch that has a design upon their butter.

However, there was a rather macabre charm, perhaps with undertones of witchcraft, which might be used to guarantee the success of the dairy and the churn. This involved stirring the milk round and round seven times with the hand of a corpse, while the person holding the dead hand repeated the incantation 'Gather, Gather, Gather.'

Lady Wilde told the following tale of a woman who was suspected of witchcraft:

> They determined to watch and find out the secret, and one day a girl from the neighbourhood, when the woman was out, got in through a chimney and hid herself under the bed, waiting there patiently till the churning began. At last, in came the woman and, having carefully closed the door, began to work with the milk, churning in the usual way without any strange doings that might seem to have magic in them. But presently she stopped and, going over to a box, unlocked it and from this receptacle, to the girl's horror, she drew forth the hand of a dead man with which she stirred the milk round and round seven times, going down on her knees and muttering an incantation all the while. Seven times she stirred the milk with the dead hand and seven times she went round the churn on her knees muttering that strange charm. After this she rose up and began to gather the butter from the churn with the dead hand, filling a pail with as much butter as the milk of ten cows. When the pail was quite full she dipped the dead hand three times in the milk, then dried it and put it back again in the box.

The girl, as soon as she could get away unperceived, fled in horror from the room and spread the news amongst the people. At once, a crowd gathered round the house with angry cries and threats to break down the door to search for the dead hand. At last the woman appeared, calm and cold as usual, and told them they were making a deal of trouble about nothing, for there was no dead hand in the house. However, the people rushed in and searched, but all they saw was a huge fire in the hearth, though the smell of burning flesh was distinctly perceptible and by this they knew she had burned the dead hand. Yet this did not save her from the vengeance of her neighbours. She was shunned by everyone; no one would eat with her or drink with her or talk to her, and after a while she and her husband quitted the island.

Those involved in witchcraft held the dew at this time of year in high regard:

If an old woman be seen gathering it in a sheet or with a sieve or with her hands upon a May Morning, nothing will persuade people that she is not performing a charm by which she can steal the butter of all the cows that graze upon the pasture from which she selects it.

When engaged in these less than neighbourly activities, the witch sometimes used the formula: *'Is liomsa leath do chod-sa'* (Half of yours is mine). One way of counteracting such spells was to follow the cow along the boreen to the field and gather the clay that her foot had touched – this rendered the cow invulnerable to the wiles and wizardry of malevolent witches. If these and other precautions were not taken, the farmer was at the mercy of dew-gatherers and chanters of spells.

Guileless and unsuspecting persons were often at risk on May Day:

Once while the churning was making in one house there, an old man came in and lighted his pipe with a cinder. After he went, they were unable to make the butter, and for many weeks they experienced the same failure. At length, a priest was called and they made another attempt, and who came in but their old man friend and he went to light his pipe a second time. The priest ordered him throw that cinder into the churn and instantly big lumps of butter appeared.

Cattle were also driven through the dying embers of the midsummer bonfire. In some areas furze bushes were set alight and these were used to herd the cattle about the field on Midsummer's Eve. Alternatively, the blazing bushes might be held over the cattle while the ashes or embers were brought home to the milking area to ensure a bountiful supply of milk for the coming year.

As we saw in the chapter on Animals in Irish Mythology, the cow had its origins in the sea. It seems appropriate, therefore, that there are many tales in Irish folklore of cows from the sea, similar to the horse tales recounted earlier:

> There was a man there long ago and he was very rich. All of a sudden he got poor. All his cows and calves died but one cow, and after a while she died too. Then he had no milk or anything. One fine morning he was out walking and he saw a fine blue cow standing outside in the *bán* [grassland]. He went and asked his wife what should he do. The wife told him to put her into the cow house and he did. When he came in, he told his wife to milk her. The wife went milking her and she had two big pails of milk. After nine months she had calves. In a year again he was as rich as ever. The neighbours were surprised how did he get rich so soon. One day one of the neighbours came in and asked where did he get the fine cow, so he told the whole story and he said he would be rich forever now. The next morning he heard the cow bellowing outside in the bán and the calves with her. He ran out after her but the cow and the calves ran away out into the sea and were seen no more.

The fairies owned white cows and the following is an example of a very popular tale which explained the appearance of the first black cow:

> In times of old it is said the fairies used to play about the borders of an Irish lake. Every fairy used to drive before her a white cow whose coat shone like silver. One day a cow strayed from the fairy herd and was caught by an old farmer. He found her amongst his own cows and liked her colour very much which was new to him. In those early times we are told that the colour of all Irish cows was a mixture of red and white, only fairy cows were pure white. There was not a black cow to be seen in Ireland. The milk of the white cows made silly people clever but the old man was not very clever. He said he would kill her for meat. The butcher arrived with his axe. They tied the cow with ropes, but before the butcher could strike a single blow, a voice was heard on the hill slope close by. 'Arise and come here,' she cried, and the white cow rose up in the air and all her calves rose. It seemed, however, that just one of the calves did not hear the voice. But when the farmer looked at her

she turned jet black. This they said was the first black cow ever seen in Ireland.

The sleek and diminutive black Kerry breed is in fact the only native Irish breed of cattle. White cows were suspect as there was always the possibility that they might return to the good people, at least to be milked. Not only did the fairies come forth to steal potatoes, the wily rascals also lured cows into the fort at milking time:

> A Kerry cow belonging to a certain family had the habit of going to the fort to be milked. Someone advised the father of the household to go to the fort and demand the spancel which had been stolen by the fairies. He did so and regained the spancel. The cow never left the farmyard to be milked after that.

The fairies, however, were not always so co-operative, and sometimes the assistance of the priest was required, as in the case of the poor man whose cow had been abducted by the fairies who resided in the fort on his land.When the priest went into the fort, he saw an ugly old woman rocking a child in a cradle. He asked her for the cow but she refused to part with the animal. The priest moved towards the cow, took a fistful of earth in his hands and threw it at her. Then he led the cow from the fort despite the protestations and maledictions of the hag. It then became the custom for the priest to walk three times around the field each night reciting prayers from a missal. The priest continued with this for about a month until one night he saw a crowd of fairies carrying an old man into the fort with them, and he went there no more thereafter.

The fairies might sometimes be quite benevolent, however:

> There was once a prosperous farmer named Richard, and he had fifteen cows, but then one by one his cows died until he had only one left, a black spotted cow. He had observed that before each of his cows had died they had been grazing in the fort. Now, however, he was determined to keep his last cow from entering the fort, but when he was taking her from the field about the fort he encountered a little man who insisted he could not take her because she belonged to the fairies. The two of them argued for a little while and the little man led him down an underground staircase so that they might settle matters. Here they came upon a huge crowd dancing to the music of a great fiddler. Now Richard was one of the good old Irish dancers so he asked the fiddler if he would oblige him with a hornpipe and he danced his fill. Then he put his hand in his pocket and gave two pence to the fiddler for his trouble. The

little man came over to him again and told him to take home the cow because he was worthy of her. They exchanged compliments. Richard took the cow home with him and the following year she had two heifer calves. Very soon Richard was a prosperous man again.

Sometimes when the fairies took a cow they might offer the lucky owner a bag of gold as payment for the animal. Nevertheless, houses or cowhouses built on fairy paths were always unlucky. Strange noises might be heard around the house or in the dairy during the course of the night. One poor man who was thus afflicted and who was suffering inexplicable losses with his butter and milk went to the priest and told him his story. Very often he had found his pans of milk disturbed and spots of blood in the churn. The priest decided to say Mass for him, and from that on all went well.

When all the cows lay down in the field it was a sign of rain; when they were harried by midges in summer time this was also a sign of rain. Porcupines or hedgehogs were an unwelcome sight in the pasturelands for they, like the hag hares, were adept at milking cows and carrying off the luck of the dairy with them.

The first, second and third days of April were called the days of the old cow: Philip Céad Bó had an old white cow. On the first of April she cocked her tail and went gadding and said: 'March is over. I'll go trying for grass.' She went too quickly and fell into a brook and was drowned. So, the first day she was drowned, the second day she was pulled out, and the third day she was buried. In some places this period was known as '*Laethanta na Bó Rabách*' (The days of the reckless cow), and in other places simply as the borrowed days. The old cow said that she would live another year now that March had passed, for the inclement winds of March usually killed anything that was old and feeble, but March resolved to bring down her pride and so he borrowed three days from April and killed the cow. On these three days people were recommended to take great care of their cattle in the fields lest they should meet the fate of the old white cow.

The bull featured in many folktales too and the following tale is one example of the most popular type, since it cast the bull in a benign role:

Once upon a time there lived a rich gentleman. He had only one son and his wife died. He got married again and his second wife became jealous of the boy and she wanted to starve him. When he was but four years old she made him mind the cows.

He had only one friend in the world, a *buláinín bán*, a little white bull. One day he was minding the cows and he got very hungry. The buláinín came over to him and told him to get on his back. The little boy did so. The buláinín told him to put his hand into his (the bull's) left ear and that he would get a cloth there, and to spread it on the ground and to ask for food. The little boy did so. He asked for food and every kind of food he wanted appeared on the cloth. He used to do this every day.

The little boy got very fat and the stepmother did not know where he was getting the food. She sent out the servant girl to watch him. The girl told her all that happened. Then the step-mother pretended to be very sick and very bad. All the doctors failed to cure her. She said after a while that nothing would cure her but the soup of the buláinín bán. The man said no, that the buláinín bán was the only playmate the boy had, but the woman let on to be very bad, and at last the man consented to kill the buláinín bán. The buláinín bán was enchanted. He told the boy that he was to be killed. He said: 'They will take me into the yard and tie me to a stake with strong chains. Let you stand by my side and when the butcher will raise the hatchet let you get on my back.'

The day came. He was tied in the yard. The butcher got ready. The old stepmother had to be brought in an armchair with joy to see him being killed. Just as the butcher was raising the hatchet, the boy jumped on the buláinín's back. The bull broke the chains and struck the woman and killed her. Then the bull galloped away, the boy on his back. The men followed on horseback. When they were very close to them the buláinín said to the boy to take a bit of wood from his ear and to throw it over his shoulder. A big wood grew up behind them. The men had to return to get saws and hatchets to cut down the wood to pass. They galloped on, and when the men were very close again, the buláinín said to the boy, 'There is a drop of water in my other ear. Throw it back over my left shoulder.' The boy did it and a lake formed and all the men were drowned.

The buláinín bán and the boy went into a wood and were living very happily. One day they heard a wild bull roaring. The white bull got afraid and said to the boy: 'Put your hand on my back. If my back is slippery I will kill him but if my back is curly he will kill me.' His back was slippery so he told the boy to get up on a tree and watch the fight. The buláinín bán killed the wild bull, and the second day he heard a bull roaring and he said: 'I must fight this bull. If my back is slippery I will kill him but if my back is curly he will kill me.' His back was curly. The boy began to cry. 'Oh,' said the bull, 'don't cry. I will leave you all my strength. Cut a belt of skin from the tip of my nose to the tip of my tail.' The boy wore this skin. Then he went looking for work.

On the way he came to a forge. He asked the smith for work. The boy said he would stay for five years if the smith would make a sword five hundred weight. 'Alright,' said the smith. When the five years were over, the sword was made. The boy caught it and he said: 'It is too light.' He said he would stay two years more if the smith made the sword seven hundred weight. When the two years were over the sword was made. 'I think this will do' said the boy. Away with him to a gentleman's house. He asked for work. The gentleman said: 'What work could you do?'

'I could mind cows grand.'

'But be sure,' says the gentleman, 'that you will not leave the cows into the giant's demesne.' These giants used to crow every morning and that crow used to be heard all over the country. One of the giants had two heads, another had three heads and the third had five heads. Everyone was very much afraid of these giants. The boy went away minding the cows for a couple of days. One day he drove his spear through the wall of the giants' demesne and drove in his cows there. They were not long there when the giant with two heads come. He said, 'You little wretch. What made you leave the cows into my land? I will kill you.'

The boy answered: 'That and your best will come together.' The two of them began to fight. The boy drove the giant to his knees into the ground, and the next twist he drove him to his hips into the ground, and the giant roared for mercy: that he would give the boy a grand suit of clothes and a white steed that would outstrip the wind. The boy said, 'I will have them and your two heads together', hitting him a blow of his sword that killed him. The same fate awaited the other two giants.

Three days later, the mother of the giants came. She was a witch and the hair of her head would harrow the ground. She had nails like steel and she fought the boy, but at last the boy killed her. Then the boy went into the castle and got all that was there.

Every seven years a fiery dragon would come on the strand, and someone should be there to be carried by him. This time it was to be the gentleman's daughter. The day came, and at twelve o'clock the girl was sitting on a chair on the strand. All the people were mourning over the fate of the gentleman's daughter. As the fiery dragon was coming out, the boy went over all the people with a black steed and drove the dragon back into the sea. He galloped back over the people and no one could catch him. The following day the daughter was there again. The gentleman told her to try and catch the boy if he came there. He did come again and he drove the fiery dragon back into the sea, and the dragon disappeared forever. There was fire out of his mouth and out of his eyes as he went. The girl went to catch the boy as he returned but she only caught his shoe and it came off in her hand. No one knew the boy as he dashed through the crowd so fast. The gentleman said that whoever the shoe would fit should be married to his daughter.

The shoe was tried on all the young men but it would fit nobody. At last someone said that it was not tried on the little cow boy. The shoe fitted him grand, and he was married to the gentleman's daughter and they lived happily. And if they don't drink coffee that we may drink tay, and if they don't live happy that we may.

If a cow had twin calves, misfortune would come to the house that year, especially if they were bull calves. Sometimes the afterbirth of a cow that had given birth was hung in the rafters of the stall to bring luck to the stock. When a cow calved a blessed candle was lighted and the Sign of the Cross made over her. The householder might also singe the hair on the udder of a newly calved cow. Sometimes when a calf was born, it was said, there might be a little bit of flesh in its mouth which it had been sucking before it came into the world. It was said that this little bit of flesh was very lucky and, if a person chanced to find it, he or she should not throw it away but hang it on the cowhouse wall. If a calf developed *Ruathar Péisteanna*, an attack of worms, he would swell up, fall to the ground and start kicking. There was apparently no orthodox cure for this disease but there was a very colourful folk cure. This cure was effected with a cord and was called *Snaidhm na Péiste* (The worm's knot). The man put the cord in the right hand over the one in the left and made another loop. He put one end of the cord into the first loop and pulled the two ends of the cord. If the cord came out without knotting, the calf would be cured, but if it did not the calf was incurable. If the knot came out, the calf would get up after a little while and run about the place.

It was believed that if a cow broke her horn, the owner should take a cobweb and place it around the horn. This would stop the bleeding and would help in the healing process. Skin complaints were treated with an application of train oil to which two or three spoonfuls of sulphur had been added. The red murrain or red water occurs in cattle when a parasite invades the red cells in the animals' blood, releasing the haemoglobin into the blood stream. One cure was to cut and boil nettles and then serve the nettle water to the animal suffering from the red murrain.

There was an interesting folk cure for Black Quarter: The farmer made a small incision in the *priocaill*, that is the long loose dewlap flesh under the cow's throat. He then inserted a slender lightly tarred rope, and made a knot on each end so that the rope would remain in position and would not fall from the dewlap. This would prevent the cow from developing the Black Quarter. When an animal died of Black Quarter, however, the diseased quarter was hewn from the dead carcass, and suspended high in the chimney from an iron hook which had been driven into the chimney wall specially for that purpose. It was believed that while this diseased quarter remained in the chimney, exposed to smoke and soot, that no other animal on the farm would succumb to the Black Quarter. This practice was surely more colourful than effective, although it found favour right throughout the country.

If a cow suffered from a disease called The *Boilg*, which apparently involved a good deal of coughing, the farmer took a threshed sheaf of corn and hung it over the smoke of the fire in the chimney for a little while. Then he took it down, set it alight and placed it under the cow's nostrils, the cow having been tethered with a short rope. The smoke from the burning sheaf was inhaled until at length, tears fell from the cow's eyes and mouth which caused her to sneeze and snort and, as this was part of the curative process, she was soon cured of the *Boilg*. In some parts, mossy sods or *scraitheanna* were burned under the animals' heads. A cure for a flagged or hard udder was to bathe it with a lather of soap and hot water until it became soft again. Fresh lard, green olive oil or blue ointment were alternative choices. Lime water might be given to a cow that had developed milk fever after calving, or she might only be 'half-milked' each day as this was believed to keep the air from getting into her udder, which caused the milk fever.

Internal worms might be treated with an unpalatable solution of soot dissolved in hot water, which was given to the animal to drink a few times a day. If a cow had sprained her leg and the leg had become badly swollen, one rather drastic remedy was to lance the shoulder and close the wound with a cleft stick. An infection in the foot was treated with archangel tar, though a rather colourful application of lard and bluestone (copper sulphate) was used in some places. Ivy leaves and fresh lard boiled together, served as a cure for itch, when rubbed to the skin. An ivy leaf was hung in the chimney when the cow had a sore eye; when the leaf disintegrated with the heat of the fire the eye would be cured.

In some areas it was held important not to spill a single drop of milk when milking a cow. In other areas, however, it was suggested that the first 'spring' from the cow should be allowed to fall on the ground for the good people. If milk was accidentally spilled, the farmer or housewife could take consolation from the fact that one of the good people would have some use for it. If a black dog without a single white hair on its body went into a dairy, no butter would be had from the milk.

The best method of preventing cows from being overlooked was to tie a red string to the tail. When this precaution was not taken and the animal was overlooked, the owner should write the name of the animal backwards on a piece of paper, and burn the paper under the animal's nose. Another method was to take a piece of clothing – the tiniest scrap – worn by the person believed to have overlooked the animal and burn it by holding it in the tongs in the fire. Whitethorn trees were generally held to be unlucky, and a cow that spent too much of her time in the shadow of a whitethorn tree was very often milked by unseen hands. It was very unlucky to bring whitethorn into the house on or after May Day. Some accounts relate that this tradition derived from the belief that Our Lord was crowned on Good Friday with thorns from the whitethorn. Sometimes an animal might be fairy-struck and one of the best methods of counteracting this malevolent influence was to pass a red hot coal over and under the body of the affected animal, singeing the hair along the back. Very often the local 'cow doctor' or folk doctor was called to diagnose and treat the condition and he sometimes substantiated his theory that the animal had been fairy-struck by producing a specimen of the dart or arrow used by the malevolent little rascals. These darts were generally remnants of stone age tools. Paradoxically, these arrow heads were sometimes used as amulets or charms to protect the cows. In some areas the fairies were especially active on Fridays, so cattle were watched with greater vigilance than ever on that day.

There were also some traditions associated with the sticks used to herd the cattle. It was considered very lucky to drive the cows to their pasture on May Day with a willow or sally rod. This would ensure a plentiful supply of milk throughout the year that followed. All year round it was held to be very unlucky, in some parts, to bring back the stick with which the cattle had been herded into the field. The stick should be tossed after the cows. It was also unlucky to strike a young animal with an alder stick, as this stunted its growth forever.

'To every cow her calf, to every book its copy', is a celebrated proverb, and was one of the first, if not the very first, statement of copyright laws anywhere in the world. St Columcille made a copy of a manuscript created by St Finian, and the dispute then arose between them about the ownership of the copy. King Diarmuid gave his judgment in favour of St Finian circa AD 560. More widely known are proverbs such as: 'Faraway cows have long horns' and 'It was often the man with three cows overtook the man with ten'. Those who indulged in idle gossip were reminded: 'By their tongues people are caught; by their horns cattle.' It was also said that a man with no cow had no need of a scythe while a man without a dog had to do his own barking. Warts were held to be lucky because the one who had them would own a cow in later years for each wart displayed. The cow featured in riddles too: 'When was beef at the highest?: When the cow jumped over the moon'; 'In and out like a trout; slippery wet and greasy: A cow's tongue'; 'Four sticks standing four little landers, two lookers, two crookers and a wheel-about: A cow'; 'What goes out a gap before a cow?: Her breath'; 'A polly cow tied to the wall, she drinks all she gets and eats nothing at all: An oil lamp'; 'A hopper of ditches, a cutter of corn, a little brown cow without a horn: A hare.'

A cow might be said to be a cooby if her horns were turned inwards. Cows that were dappled were said to be sprecket or bracky, *breac* being the Irish word for dappled. When animals were sold at the fair the buyer was entitled to luck money. This was generally called the luck penny and ranged from a shilling per calf to 3 shillings per cow in the late 1930s. The luck penny was also mandatory when eggs for hatching were sold, otherwise the buyer would have no luck with his or her eggs. The best cure for a burn was to apply cow dung to it, because the cow was believed to eat the most wholesome grasses and herbs.

* * *

Other Creatures: 'I move without wings between silk strings / I leave as you find my substance behind: A spider.' A spider's web was used to stop the bleeding when a cow broke her horn. One day the soldiers were hunting Mary and Joseph and the Christ Child. The Holy Family had taken refuge in a cave and Mary prayed to God when she heard the rhythmic pounding of the soldiers' footsteps coming closer and closer. A spider came and hurriedly wove a great web about the entrance, and seconds later, when one of the soldiers suggested they should search the cave, the captain pointed to the web and said that no one had entered the cave in years. This was how the spider saved the Christ Child, His Mother and St Joseph, and that is why it is very unlucky to kill a spider, one of the most popular beliefs of my own childhood.

If one had a toothache one remedy was to place a live frog in the mouth. Alternatively, one might chew a frog's leg. Here is a story about a frog:

> Long ago there was a midwife. One day she was out in the field and she kicked a frog with her boot when she happened to see it in the grass. She went to bed that night but she was not long in bed when she heard a rap at the door and she opened it. There was a man outside with a horse. He spoke to her and said, 'Come along with me.' He placed a blindfold over her eyes and put her on the horse's back. They went on until they came to a house. She went into the house, where the blindfold was removed, and she saw a woman sick in bed, and she had to stay there with her until she was better. She returned home with a black patch in her side so that she might suffer as the frog had suffered.

The clear implication of this little tale was that the woman the midwife was required to tend had been one and the same as the frog she had kicked during the day.

If a swarm of bees came to your house from another person's house, you should never allow them to be taken back, even if you knew the owner, for if this happened the luck of the year would go with the bees. When someone died and the house was in mourning the bees should be told all about the death, and a piece of black crepe encircled round the hive. If this were not done the bees would refuse to make their honey and would simply pine away and die.

It was considered lucky to have crickets singing in the hearth. They were enchanted creatures and their singing generally served to keep away the fairies who were quite partial to sitting around the fire at night when the people of the house had gone to bed. It was very unlucky to kill a cricket, for the deceased's relatives might take it upon themselves to make holes in your socks or woollen garments. I often heard the crickets sing in the hearth in an old farmhouse set high on a mountainside overlooking the deep and secluded valley called *An Chúm Dhubh*, The Black Valley, which lies beyond the Gap of Dunloe in County Kerry. If a neighbour or stranger killed a cricket they might desert the hearth for a time and set off to wreak their vengeance on the malefactor in question. Crickets, like their human overlords, were very partial to wakes and funerals. When one of their number died they came together and had a grand wake, and it was surely at these wakes that it was determined whether the passing of the dearly departed had been the result of natural causes or murderous intent on the part of some ill-bred human in the vicinity.

If the cricket was liked, the cockroach and the daradaol were despised. My mother often told how the daradaol had betrayed Christ to the soldier. Our Lord had just passed through a field but the soldiers had come to the conclusion that they had lost track of him. 'Nay, nay Jesus crossed the field,' said the daradaol, and since that time the daradaol was cursed. I later discovered that in some areas it was held that you would gain an indulgence if you made an end of the hapless daradaol. The correct procedure was to kill it with the nail of your thumb. In some versions of the story, the *ciaróg* (beetle) intervened and shouted at the daradaol. 'You lie, you lie,' which explains why the *ciaróg* should not be molested.

The ladybird was the gardener's friend, and was always treated with respect. There were many nonsense rhymes about animals and here is just one:

> Thirteen lambs in a nest with their tails cocked to the west;
> Twelve ladies in a ring, six to dance and six to sing;
> Eleven transmogrified ministers in a pulpit preaching,
> Ten horses well shorn and shod, their tails and manes in good
>   order.
> Nine cows milking and their spancels made of silk,
> Eight nanny hammers in an oven dancing.
> Seven squirkin squirrels in a crooked crab tree squealing,
> Six grey geese in a green field grazing.
> Five pigger-riggers in a rye field rooting,
> Four hare hedlers, three plump partridges,
> Two ducks and a fat hen.'

In the world of modern agriculture very often there is little time for folk tradition and folk cures, but such traditions represent a colourful strand in the weave that is Irish heritage.

TALES OF IRISH ENCHANTMENT
Patricia Lynch

Patricia Lynch brings to this selection of classical Irish folktales for young people all the imagination and warmth for which she is renowned.

There are seven stories here: Midir and Etain, The Quest of the Sons of Turenn, The Swan Children, Deirdre and the Sons of Usna, Labra the Mariner, Cuchulain – The Champion of Ireland and The Voyage of Maeldun.

They lose none of their original appeal in the retelling and are as delightful today as when they were first told.

The stories are greatly enhanced by the immediacy and strength of Frances Boland's imaginative drawings.

ENCHANTED IRISH TALES
Patricia Lynch

Enchanted Irish Tales tells of ancient heroes and heroines, fantastic deeds of bravery, magical kingdoms, weird and wonderful animals... This new illustrated edition of classical folktales, retold by Patricia Lynch with all the imagination and warmth for which she is renowned, rekindles the age-old legends of Ireland, as exciting today as they were when first told. The collection includes:

- Conary Mór and the Three Red Riders
- The Long Life of Tuan Mac Carrell
- Finn Mac Cool and Fianna
- Oisin and The Land of Youth
- The Kingdom of The Dwarfs
- The Dragon Ring of Connla
- Mac Datho's Boar
- Ethne

IRISH FAIRY TALES
Michael Scott

'He found he was staring directly at a leprechaun. The small man was sitting on a little mound of earth beneath the shade of a weeping willow tree... The young man could feel his heart beginning to pound. He had seen leprechauns a few times before but only from a distance. They were very hard to catch, but if you managed at all to get hold of one...'

Michael Scott's exciting stories capture all the magic and mystery of Irish folklore. This collection of twelve fairy tales, beautifully and unusually illustrated, include:

The arrival of the Tuatha de Danann in Erin

The fairy horses	The King's secret
The crow goddess	The fairies' revenge
The wise woman's payment	The shoemaker and himself
The floating island	The sunken town

IRISH ANIMAL TALES
Michael Scott

'Have you ever noticed how cats and dogs sometimes sit up and look at something that is not there? Have you ever seen a dog barking at nothing? And have you ever wondered why? Perhaps it is because the animals can see the fairy folk coming and going all the time, while humans can only see the little People at certain times...'

This illustrated collection of Michael Scott's strange stories reveal a wealth of magical creatures that inhabit Ireland's enchanted animal kingdom. The tales tell of the king of the cats, the magical cows, the fox and the hedgehog, the dog and the leprechaun, March, April and the Brindled Cow, the cricket's tale... A collection to entrance readers, both young and old.